D0460548

UNIQUE EATS AND EATERIES

OF

PORTLAND, OREGON

Copyright © 2018, Reedy Press, LLC
All rights reserved.
Reedy Press
PO Box 5131
St. Louis, MO 63139
www.reedypress.com

No part of this publication may be reproduced or transmitted in any form or by any means, electronic or mechanical, including photocopy, recording, or any information storage and retrieval system, without permission in writing from the publisher. Permissions may be sought directly from Reedy Press at the above mailing address or via our website at www.reedypress.com.

Library of Congress Control Number: 2018945704
ISBN: 9781681061863

Book Design: Barbara Northcott
Photos credit of the author unless otherwise indicated.

Printed in the United States of America
18 19 20 21 22   5 4 3 2 1

UNIQUE EATS AND EATERIES

OF

PORTLAND, OREGON

ADAM SAWYER

CONTENTS

ACKNOWLEDGMENTS

When I signed on to write this book, I thought I had a pretty keen understanding of Portland's food scene. For seven years I'd been writing about the city's food and drink for numerous outlets, while also giving a variety of culinary tours that explore every theme and quadrant. But I didn't know what I didn't know. Thanks to the story-driven approach of the Unique Eats & Eateries book series, I now possess a depth of understanding that has changed the way I see the food scene in Portland, and everywhere. A change for the better, and I wish to thank Reedy Press for the opportunity. I would also like to thank the owners, chefs, managers, and staff at every one of the restaurants discussed in this book. As a general rule, they are extremely busy people who work seemingly endless hours because, by and large, they love what they do. I thank you all for taking the time to tell me your stories, exposing occasionally uncomfortable details about your life and your journey. I wish you all continued success!

I want to thank my lovely partner, Kara, for putting up with me when I became a deadline-induced basket case, slowed mightily by project-based weight gain. Thanks to the family—Jade Sawyer Chase and the Chase family, Crystal Neeley and the Neely family, Janaira Quigley and all the Quiglets, Cindy Sawyer, and William Sawyer. Thanks to Thea Sawyer for her continued inspiration. Thanks to the friends who have supported and eaten with me over the years—Dan Wakefield, Marc Alan Jordan, Kassidy Cooprider, Anna Haller, Rebekah Voie, Stephanie Paris, Mac Barrett, and many others. Thanks to my culinary compatriot, Mattie John Bamman, for the insight, entertainment, and alcohol-fueled world-domination planning sessions. Thanks to the outstanding companies that I have had, or currently have, the honor of giving tours for—Portland Walking Tours, Evergreen Escapes, and Portland Eat Adventures. And big thanks to the outlets, editors, friends, and supporters who have helped along the way, and who continue to enable me to make this wonderful ride a career.

INTRODUCTION

The "farm-to-table" movement has been gaining momentum in this country for decades. And cities that are near prime growing regions have been flourishing in its wake. The Willamette Valley is the nation's new breadbasket, and arguably its finest growing region. Bordered on the west by the Oregon Coast Range and the Cascade Mountains to the east, a number of factors contribute to the 150-mile-long valley's agricultural attractiveness. Some standard attributes—like plenty of annual rainfall, a temperate climate that allows for year-round growing, and a handful of different ecoregions—set the table. But what really helped separate the Willamette Valley from perhaps anyplace else was a series of massive, ice-age floods.

The Missoula Floods scoured eastern Washington and Oregon before settling in the Willamette Valley. Because of these cataclysmic events, the topsoil in the area is as deep as half a mile in places. When you factor that into everything else that the valley has going for it, you get an area that is essentially a petri dish for growing produce. And thanks to the urban growth boundaries that had been established in the early 1970s, much of the valley remained preserved and pristine. Portland, Oregon, sits right at its northern end.

Compared to most other West Coast cities, Portland was also affordable. As word of these attributes began to spread, chefs and artisans came in numbers to take advantage. The influx of talent combined with world-class ingredients, affordability, and the city's creative culture produced a culinary storm that began swirling around the Willamette Valley, and Portland was at the eye of it. It wasn't long before everything else fell into place—cheesemakers, bakers, ranchers, brewers, winemakers, distillers, farmers, salumists, etc., began springing up everywhere, setting the bar for dining expectations ever higher.

However, the food scene is composed of far more than artisanal farm-to-table fare. Bars and brewpubs have been catering to the tastes of their respective neighborhoods with aplomb, long before the words *local* and *seasonal* became part of the lexicon. The watering holes in Portland serve everything from hangover-curing plates of beige comfort to proper British pub fare and even elevated offerings that you would never expect to see from an establishment that also sports karaoke and a trivia night. Do not overlook the bar food in Portland.

Somewhere in between the local dive bars and the restaurants anchored by James Beard Award winners is a space occupied by the food carts. Arguably the most unique facet of eating in Portland, the food-cart culture here is quite different from that of the food trucks that are making waves in just about every other city at the moment. Thanks to some permissive city ordinances, the carts legally have to be mobile, but they don't necessarily need to be. As a consequence, they typically conjugate into stationary pods throughout town— including neighborhood collections that in some cases are the social hub of the community. They feature predominantly ethnic food, but they go well beyond Mexican and Thai, covering Filipino, Russian, Indian, Mauritian, and then some. They also serve as a proving ground or farm league for chefs. At last count, more than twenty food carts have gone on to become brick-and-mortar restaurants.

The cuisine scene in Portland is also complemented by an equally powerful set of liquid assets. Between the wine, beer, distilled spirits, cider, and mead, there is no way you can't get artisanally hammered in this town. Put it all together and Portland takes a culinary back seat to no other city in America. This book is a collection of the people, places, and stories that made it what it is today—and will have a hand in what it morphs into tomorrow.

UNIQUE EATS AND EATERIES

OF

PORTLAND, OREGON

Excellent contemporary Creole cuisine with an amazing backstory. *Closed*

Many stories penned in Hollywood have more believable plots than the true-life story of Tapalaya chef/owner Anh Luu. After the Vietnam War, Luu's parents moved to New Orleans. She was born and raised into a Creole world within a thriving Vietnamese community. The Asian Cajun cuisine Chef Luu grew up with was not necessarily what many people today would refer to as fusion. It is an evolved sub-species of the already ethnically collaborative genus, Creole. New Orleans has a long-established Vietnamese community that makes Cajun food incorporating Vietnamese ingredients. For example—Chef Luu's own Crawfish Étouffée includes roasted chiles, lemongrass, and shrimp paste. She grew up in and around restaurants, making everything from scratch. This was Anh Luu's life, and at the tender age of fifteen, she knew she wanted to be a chef. Working the line was no easy task in the male-dominated restaurant world. But talent and hard work have a way of rising above, despite the obstacles. Her career was on track until 2009, when Hurricane Katrina hit the area. Nineteen-year-old Luu and her family lost everything.

Her parents moved to Portland to start over, and she went to college in New Orleans. She bounced around a bit before finally making the move out to Portland herself. She worked front-of-the-house restaurant jobs for a while before deciding to attend the

Anh Luu had a viral hit in 2017 when the website Eater Portland featured her now-legendary Pho-rrito, the marriage of a burrito and Vietnamese Pho, in one of its videos.

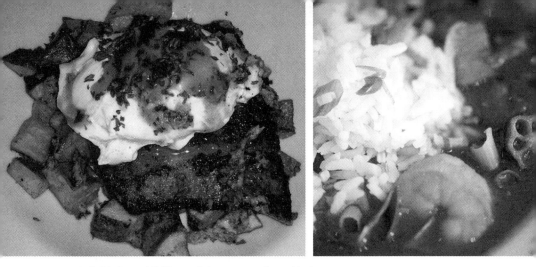

Left: Blackened Halibut with Lemongrass Pesto Hash.
Right: Gumbo at Tapalaya.

Western Culinary Institute. Upon completing her training, she worked stints at a few legendary Portland institutions, including Mother's Bistro and Tanuki. She even worked briefly at Tapalaya (a combination of the words *tapas* and *jambalaya*) between Mother's and Tanuki gigs before returning to Tapalaya do some consulting for the restaurant. She eventually took over the role of executive chef. In 2017, Chef Luu purchased Tapalaya.

Today, the restaurant continues to thrive under Luu's direction. She sources the best local ingredients she can find to put out palate- and genre-expanding offerings like her Boudin Sausage Eggrolls. In addition to the Asian Cajun dishes of her youth, she produces straight Creole standards like red beans & rice along with some classic Asian-inspired offerings. In the future, she hopes to perhaps incorporate some elevated French influence as well. But for now, few things tickle Chef Luu as much as when old men from Louisiana claim that her Crawfish Étouffée is the best they've ever had. It tastes like home, they say—there's just a little something extra there. Something spectacular, but they can never quite put their finger on it.

28 Northeast 28th Ave.
503-232-6652
tapalaya.com

A proper English pub in Southeast Portland.

"If it were any more authentic, you'd need a passport." So proclaims at least one of the unofficial mottos of Southeast Portland's beloved Horse Brass Pub. And you'll receive no argument from anyone who has ever passed through its doors. It's dark wood, darts, proper pints, ploughman's platters, and fish & chips. As an English-style pub, it's unparalleled in the Northwest and perhaps even further afield, receiving recognition for its aesthetic, ambiance, food, and beer from the *New York Times*, *Esquire*, and the Food Channel, among others. But the Horse Brass has become legendary for more than its legitimacy as a pub. It is one of Old Portland's last remaining institutions—a hallowed den that helped launch Oregon's craft beer scene.

The history of the Horse Brass has been told many times, and while some of the details might muddle, the basic facts have remained intact. In 1976, Don Younger sat in an unassuming Belmont pub while his car was being worked on at an auto shop

Business partner Joellen Piluso is proud that the Horse Brass remains a place that exemplifies Old Portland–a place where people still talk to each other instead of looking at their phones, money wasn't the most important thing, and deals are sealed with a handshake. It's always been that way. In fact, a young man from Seattle who was working for the Youngers back in the late '90 s was in need of some cash to help his fledgling business get off the ground. Don gave him the money over a pint and a handshake, and that young man, Duane Sorenson, used the money to open Stumptown Coffee.

You've got options.

across the street. One pint turned into six, and as the day evolved
into evening, Younger began drinking with the then-owner of the
Horse Brass, Jay Brandon. The next morning, Younger discovered
a bill of sale for the pub scribbled on a napkin. His brother and
business partner, Bill, was less than enthused when Don broke the
news to him. But the two were now in this thing together, so they
went about the business of making the Horse Brass the best pub
they could.

Much of the decor was already in place, but to help with the details
and food menu, the Younger brothers brought in UK expats Betty
and Brian Dutch. With soccer on TV, darts in the corner, and scotch
eggs, bangers, and pasties on the menu, it didn't take long for the
Brass to become home away from home for British transplants and
locals alike. And then there was the beer. Don Younger was a died-
in-the-wool Blitz beer man. Eventually, Don was convinced to try a
Bass Ale, and his palate began to expand. The Youngers broadened

the tap selection to include an array of imports. Then, as craft beer began its groundswell in the '80s the Youngers championed the cause of Oregon breweries as well as some others that would later become cornerstones of craft beer in America. They consulted with and poured beers from Widmer Brothers, Rogue, Deschutes, Sierra Nevada, BridgePort, and Russian River, to name a few. In 1989, Rogue produced a house beer especially for the Horse Brass, a special bitter that was nameless until the unexpected death of Bill Younger. The beer was named in his honor, and to this day you can still order a pint of William Younger's Special Bitter, or YSB, which is always on tap. Or get a "Billy," if you prefer it cask-conditioned.

4534 Southeast Belmont St.
503-232-2202
horsebrass.com

Top: Inside Portland's favorite pub.

Left: Walking into the Horse Brass.

The rebirth and reenvisioning of a Portland institution.

Some people are blessed to know what they are going to do with their lives from an early age. Chef Annie Cuggino is one of them. Growing up on Long Island, she spent as much time as possible in the kitchen. So once high school was finished, she went off to the Culinary Institute of America in New York. She thrived on the training and camaraderie. When she completed school, a chef friend of hers tipped her off that the Union Square Cafe needed a prep cook, and just like that, she had her first real restaurant job.

It was a formative time for Cuggino. Watching the way Chef Michael Romano ran his kitchen and treated his staff had a big impact on her. It was difficult, but Cuggino thrived again, eventually working her way up to the grill station. That's where she was when *New York Times* restaurant critic Bryan Miller visited the Union Square Cafe. Romano didn't push her aside; on the contrary, he allowed her to shine, and the cafe was elevated to three stars. Cuggino eventually moved to New Orleans, where she worked with Emeril Lagasse for a brief time before deciding to strike out on her own in Portland. She worked a couple of gigs around town before accepting the position of executive chef at Veritable Quandary (VQ).

At the time, it was a bit of a step backwards for Cuggino. The historic 1st Avenue pub wasn't known for its food. It was a cozy place where businessmen went for cocktails after work. But over the next twenty-two years, she turned VQ into a bona fide Portland culinary landmark. Her success can be attributed to a number of factors, including talent, drive, impeccable palate, the magic of a historic building, and, undoubtedly, the way she collaborates with her team. Cuggino relies on her kitchen staff's diverse backgrounds and talents. She empowers them to contribute and share ideas. It had become a

Left: Dessert.
Right: Chef Annie Cuggino.

restaurant family firing on all cylinders when she got the news: The VQ building was to be torn down and replaced with a courthouse. Cuggino, her staff, and the city of Portland were collectively at a loss.

A longtime customer at VQ asked Cuggino if she would be interested in opening a new restaurant, just a few blocks away. It was a no brainer, but the timing had to be right. She wanted to keep her team intact. So they built out a beautiful new space with a large, open kitchen that would be ready for business in short order. And three weeks after the closing of Veritable Quandary, Cuggino and her staff opened Q. The larger space has enabled her to keep the classics while simultaneously broadening the menu's scope. Q was an immediate success, picking up where VQ left off and building upon it. It was a nervous transition for Cuggino, however. She wasn't sure how much of her prosperity was tied to the ghosts of the old building. But almost two years into Q, it's become evident that the magic had been woven by her and her restaurant family all along.

828 Southwest 2nd Ave.
503-850 8915
q-portland.com

As these words are being typed, Peter Vuong is a semifinalist for the James Beard Award for Best Chef Northwest. His Vietnamese family restaurant, Ha VL, is a nondescript hole-in-the-wall within the Wing Ming Market Center. It's not the type of establishment that typically curries favor with the James Beard Foundation. But it's more than the restaurant's unassuming location and appearance that make its story a movie-worthy underdog tale. Far more.

During the Vietnam War, Peter Vuong's father, William, served as a Provincial Reconnaissance Forces Commander working in cooperation with the CIA. But the new communist regime didn't appreciate his work with the United States when the war ended. As a result, William Vuong was sentenced to ten years in a Vietnamese prison. This left Peter's mother, Christina Ha Luu, alone to raise six boys during a very turbulent time. Upon William's release, his wife and four of the six boys, including Peter, fled to find a safe place for the family. They ended up in a Malaysian refugee camp on Bidong Island in the South China Sea. Conditions, by all accounts, were horrific. The four sons were able to come to the United States in 1986, having been sponsored for immigrant status by one of William's former students. But even with the four boys in the US, William Vuong and Christina were unable to obtain refugee status themselves and settled in Saigon. Finally, seven years later, they were granted entry into the United States. More than a decade after that, the family's dream of opening its own restaurant came true in the form of Ha VL in 2006.

Business was slow at first. The new restaurant served primarily coffee and sandwiches. But when Christina began to integrate soup recipes passed on to her by her mother and mother-in-law, things picked up significantly. Peter Vuong took over Ha VL from his parents when they retired. Finding that they weren't suited for

Left: Turmeric Yellow noodle
Right: Beef Pho

inactivity, William and Christina open another restaurant, Rose VL. Now Peter, along with his own family, maintain the high standards for the restaurant set by his mother. Ha VL serves a rotating menu of two soups a day until they sell out. If you're thinking of coming in any time after 1 p.m., don't bother. Plan on being hungrier earlier the next day. Peter sources the best ingredients he can find, makes everything from scratch, takes no shortcuts, and serves everything fresh—which, admittedly, is easier to do when you sell out every day. Peter Vuong is honored to be nominated for an award as prestigious as James Beard Best Chef, but he's not losing any sleep over it. He has to be up pretty early to see that his soup broths are reducing properly.

2738 Southeast 82nd Ave.
503-772-0103
mrgan.com/havl

MY FATHER'S PLACE

One of the city's truly great dive bars is a place for everybody.

Portland's Central Eastside Industrial District is yet another part of town that has been undergoing massive changes as of late. And while destination dining establishments and purveyors of artisanal everything continue to pop up all around it, My Father's Place (MFP) remains more or less unchanged from the day it opened in 1978. By some estimations, MFP is a dive bar. And that would not be an inaccurate assessment. But it's also an old-school diner, knick-knack treasure trove, lounge, and game room. It is where truckers, punks, transients and transplants, the curious and the constant, poets, businessmen, couples and families have broken bread and enjoyed each other's company for all but 3½ hours of each day, 365 days a year, since the late '70s. The clientele at 6 a.m., when the restaurant opens, are just as likely to be ending their day as beginning it. Vice versa when they close at 2:30 a.m. And it is as culturally significant to this town as any of the places you'll find on a clickbait list telling you what you have to see when you come here.

Finished in 1892, the Logus building in Southeast Portland is on the National Register of Historic Places. It's also home to My Father's Place. The restaurant/bar has seen a few incarnations over the years, including a piano bar named Andy's. Merrie Ann Dillon began waitressing there in the early '80s a few years after it became

> "All ages, races, genders, sexual orientations, political views, sharing the same space, food, and drink. It has ALWAYS been that way there." Darrell Moles, co-owner, My Father's Place.

Left: Exterior of My Father's Place.
Right: Regulars at My Father's Place.

MFP. She eventually became co-owner, and then a few years later, sole proprietor. It's been a family affair for Dillon ever since, who sold the restaurant to her daughter, Linda Moles, in 2002. Moles's children, Darrell and Kasey, grew up there. On weekends they would come in and help their grandmother separate money before playing video games. In the summer, they would earn extra cash by cleaning the antiques that adorn the ceiling. Over the years everybody pitched in—Linda waitressed, Darrell tended bar, and Kasey pulled a stint in the dish pit. And the staff at MFP is an extension of the family that owns it. Of the roughly twenty-five folks on payroll at the moment, at least half of them have been there for more than five years, including Danette (Dee) with twenty years, Sarah with nineteen, Miguel with seventeen, and Carlos with eleven. The Moles family now also owns the Side Door and the Ship Ahoy Tavern—great bars in their own right. But for many Portlanders, there is only one true dive-bar melting pot, and it's My Father's Place.

523 Southeast Grand Ave.
503-235-5494
myfathersplacepdx.com

Perhaps Portland's hippest place to dine, it's much more than meets the eye.

Departure certainly lives up to its name. At first glance, it doesn't look or feel anything like Portland. Located at the top of the luxury Nines Hotel, Departure seems out of place and time, given the city of Portland's current incarnation. With its sweeping views, modern feel, and hyper-stylized staff—and clientele, for that matter—it's Los Angeles or New York. It's not very casual or rustic. Everybody is attractive, well-dressed, and perfectly perfumed. How can this be Portland? Give it a minute.

Without a doubt, Departure draws a different clientele than a lot of other top Portland restaurants. Because of its vibe, location, and reputation, it has become a destination for locals as well as out of towners looking for a next-level experience. Sure, there is an element of "see and be seen" to it. But depending on the time of night you go, you'll see happy hour suits, early dinner jeans, late-dinner dresses, and late-night getups. But hot places eventually cool down. Substance above style is required for staying power. At Departure, the style accentuates the substance, not the other way around.

Chef Gregory Gourdet has taken a bumpy but ultimately triumphant path in ascending his way to executive chef. After finding sobriety, he eventually landed at Departure. Following a three-year stint as chef de cuisine, he was promoted to executive chef and has been pushing the restaurant's modern Asian menu ever since. Not

Chef Gourdet has garnered a number of accolades through the years. But his second-place finish on season twelve of Bravo TV's *Top Chef* catapulted him to local celebrity status.

Above left: Chef Gregory Gourdet. Courtesy of Departure Restaurant + Lounge

Top right: Departure's West Deck at the top of the Nines Hotel. Courtesy of Departure Restaurant + Lounge

Above right: One of Departure's inventive sushi offerings.

afraid to think outside the box or take risks, Gourdet employs ancient techniques through modern technology. For example, food waste is minimal to non-existent at Departure. If something didn't make it to the plate on its first run, it will be pickled, fermented, or composted. From there, chances are good that the transformed former ingredient will assist a new one to thrive in the restaurant's rooftop garden. In the basement of the Nines, the food lab is where hydroponics, aeroponics, and aquaponics are all used in the production of future ingredients.

Chef Gourdet and the entire Departure staff have created a place that people go to, and not through. It's experiential. You seek it out for warm, genuinely friendly service as well as exceptional, locally sourced food that is ever evolving. They are creatively doing what they want to do, how they want to do it, outside of the way it's being done by others. And if that isn't Portland—and a departure—then nothing is.

525 Southwest Morrison South
503-802-5370
departureportland.com

Soul food restaurant with Cajun flair providing more than a great dining experience.

Pastor E. D. Mondainé grew up on soul food. The St. Louis native can easily and blissfully recall a time in his life when every member of the extended family excelled in one particular dish—a specialty he or she would bring to family gatherings, which became All-Star lineups of dinner offerings. It was food created from the soul to feed the soul. Pastor Mondainé would grow into a man who extended the tradition and meaning of soul food into just about every aspect of his life. He is a philanthropist, activist, entrepreneur, author, civic leader, musician, and now president of the Portland NAACP. Pastor Mondainé was the senior pastor at the Celebration Tabernacle in 1990 when he launched Girl & Guy Fridays, a copying and secretarial service with a cafe and predecessor to his restaurant, Po'Shines Cafe De La Soul.

Pastor Mondainé saw a need. A number of local community members on public assistance were talented but defeated by a cycle of depression, abuse, and the resulting low self-esteem that contributes to the cycle's continuation. He thought that with proper guidance, discipline, and development, he could produce

The restaurant name Po'Shines was inspired by a man named Cecil Wooden, nicknamed Po' Shine by Mayor Tom Bradley of Los Angeles. One of Wooden's desires was to get fried fish from a local restaurant that had a purpose and provided an excellent product.

Left: BBQ Ribs at Po'Shines.

Center: An Assortment of soul food sides.

Right: Delicious options for breakfasts, lunch, and dinner.

empowerment and opportunity. He was right. Girl & Guy Fridays began putting on Friday dinners that often featured live music. The events were so popular that he eventually opened Po'Shines in Kenton to accommodate the demand for the exceptional food. But Po'Shines was more than a restaurant. It became home to a new initiative, a youth work organization called "Teach Me to Fish" (TMTF). The comprehensive culinary training program provides classes and training in a well-structured environment that teaches not only culinary job skills, but also life skills necessary for success. What Po'Shines does goes even deeper than that. Pastor Mondainé elaborates: "We strive to create an environment where food can foster conversation, and where conversation can turn into life application and change. We want to open a dialogue that can create a strong community and empower individuals. More than anything, we are a people who rejuvenate our patrons and community members through our exceptional food, service, and opportunity to be part of change."

Since opening in 2007, Po'Shines and the TMTF program have expanded into multiple locations and a Culinary and Catering Clinic that offers a full eighteen-month curriculum with clinics taught by some of the city's top chefs. True to the very nature of soul food, Pastor Mondainé continues to nourish his community, in ways that go well beyond food.

8139 North Denver Ave.

503-978-9000

poshines.com

ELEPHANTS DELICATESSEN

A Portland mainstay for almost too many reasons to count.

Why can you watch grandma make a soup, take careful notes, observe subtle nuances, and be convinced that you have it down—but when it's your time to shine, you can never replicate her final product in quite the same way? Did she sneak something in while you weren't looking? Perhaps it's just an extra quarter cup of love that only she's capable of infusing. Regardless, there's certainly no way that some brick and mortar shop can swing grandma's recipe if you can't, right? Hold that thought.

Elaine Tanzer founded Elephants Delicatessen in April of 1979—a really long time ago by local food-service standards. At that time, there were no specialty food stores in Portland. There were very few in the whole country, for that matter. Inspired by the great food shops of Europe, Elephants Delicatessen became a pioneer in gourmet innovations. Because nothing could be bought in the area, she had to fly in high-quality products and ingredients from somewhere else in the states, or Europe, or figure out a way to make it herself. Elephants Deli grew and became the first to offer Portlanders fresh pasta, pesto sauce, chocolate truffles, cheeses from

A few generations of Portlanders have grown up on Elephants Delicatessen soup, and sometimes they need a taste of home. It's not uncommon for the deli to ship out quarts of the "Elephants Cure" soup all across the country to college students during flu season, as well as students who might be suffering from a bit of homesickness.

Left: Happy employees make great food at Elephants Delicatessen.
Right: A selection of soups.

around the world, fresh-squeezed orange juice, homemade bread, and fresh, ready-to-go food from a deli counter. Easy enough items to find now in Portland, but Elephants Delicatessen led the charge, while also raising the bar for quality and service.

Nearly forty years later, they've grown quite a bit. The Elephants's staff members are still doing the things they've always done, but now they do them via seven retail stores, a corporate lunch delivery program, and a catering service. Despite the size, they've maintained the magic. Elephants Delicatessen is more like a big family that loves to eat, drink, laugh, and enjoy each other's company rather than a large, profit-driven company. And the proof is in the pudding. The company remains family owned and operated. In fact, CEO/Owner Anne Weaver and Executive Chef/Owner Scott Weaver have both worked for Elephants for more

Specialty meats from across town and across the globe.

than thirty-five years. And they aren't the only employees who have been there for decades. The wine buyer has worked at Elephants for more than thirty years, and the store manager at the flagship Northwest 22nd Avenue store is celebrating twenty-five years with the company. So, maybe a brick and mortar *can* make a soup as good as grandma's. It just takes a little bit of love from a whole lot of people.

115 Northwest 22nd Ave.
503-224-3955
elephantsdeli.com

Mushroom pizza.

Indian-inspired vegan restaurant doubles as a classic Portland success story.

Sanjay Chandrasekaran is a case study in why Portland is so attractive to culinary talent. He grew up working the kitchens of Albuquerque, New Mexico. He washed dishes and did prep work for a pizza place throughout high school. When he turned 18, Chandrasekaran took another job dishwashing and doing prep, but this time he ascended the ranks to a lead line cook position. He worked various line cook jobs all through college, and after graduating he moved to Portland. Wanting to try something new, Chandrasekaran became an arborist for a few years before returning to the culinary arts. Only this time, it was in the form of his own food cart named Sonny Bowl, serving vegan bowls and smoothies at the Southwest 3rd and Washington food pod.

After a few years of feeling out the Portland food scene and securing things financially, he opened a brick and mortar restaurant, the Sudra, specializing in what Chandrasekaran calls inauthentic vegan Indian food. This allowed him to spread his wings a bit, blending Indian flavor profiles with Northwest culinary sensibilities. You're not likely to find a kale-infused dosa anywhere in India, but it will sell like hotcakes in Portland. While the Sudra was developing a following, he turned the well-established Sonny Bowl into its own brick and mortar, Rabbits Cafe. The inspiration for the name came from a would-be customer

"Some of our dishes at the Sudra are just things we made up using common Indian flavors and spices, like our black lentil kofta, chickpea cutlets, or the peacock salad. I don't think anyone is approaching Indian food this way anywhere in the world."   –Chef/Owner Sanjay Chandrasekaran

Above left: The exterior of Chandrasekaran's Sudra.

Top right: A plate of indian-inspired vegan goodness at the Sudra.

Above right: The Sudra's interior.

who declared the Sonny Bowl menu to be rabbit food. One year after that, Chandrasekaran opened the second Sudra in St. Johns.

Not wanting to rest on his laurels, in 2017 he and longtime friend and fellow food cart owner Tal Caspi opened Aviv, a vegan Israeli restaurant, in Southeast. Put it all together and you have an archetype Portland success story. Sanjay Chandrasekaran came to Portland and opened a food cart to get some skin in the game. He simultaneously demonstrated proof of concept with the cart while developing his own understanding of the region's ingredients, its inhabitants' tastes, and his own culinary voice. Then he took advantage of the city's relative affordability to open his own restaurants and collaborated with a like-minded friend to do the same. This is how Chandrasekaran became a restaurateur, and how the city of Portland became one of the best food cities in America.

2333 Northeast Glisan St.
503-302-6002
thesudra.com

COUNTRY CAT
DINNER HOUSE & BAR

A husband and wife team helped bring scratch-made American craft cooking to Portland.

Adam Sappington grew up in Missouri, initially drawn to the subconscious side of what is great about food—family. Food brought everybody together in one place to enjoy each other's company and celebrate. More often than not, the gatherings were anchored by his grandmother's fried chicken. At the age of nineteen he officially fell in love with food. He was bussing tables in Columbia, Missouri, one night when they threw him on the grill. He didn't know what he was doing, but he knew that he loved the energy, camaraderie, and creative outlet the kitchen provided. In 1994 Sappington moved to Portland sight unseen, where he worked to put himself through culinary school. After completing his training, he worked around a bit before landing a job at Wildwood, a Portland landmark. Wildwood had a familial culinary culture, and it was there that Sappington met the woman he would eventually start his own family with.

Jackie Sappington had grown up with her nose in cookbooks. She had a natural talent for baking, endeavoring her first puff pastry at the age of ten. By the time she left for college, her interest in food had come into full bloom. She attended the University of Oregon, where

In 2015, the Sappingtons competed together on the popular Food Network show *Chopped*. The episode was a special couples edition, and true to form, the Sappingtons cleared all obstacles together, claiming the title of Chopped Champions.

Left: Jackie and Adam Sappington.
Right: Cast-Iron Skillet Fried Chicken. Photo courtesy of Frances Dyer.

she studied the anthropology of food. In 1995 she moved to Portland, and without any formal culinary training she relied on repetition, resolve, and an uncanny understanding of food to work her way into some of the city's best restaurants. Including Wildwood.

According to Adam, it was love at first sight. The two built a powerful professional and personal relationship that would result in marriage five years later. The couple continued working independently in kitchens around Portland, with Jackie rededicating herself to baking and earning her pastry chops. They started a family, and when the opportunity presented itself, they opened a neighborhood restaurant in Montavilla, the Country Cat Dinner House & Bar. With Adam serving as executive chef and Jackie as executive pastry chef, the couple drew on inspiration from childhood as well as their work in Portland's best restaurants to create something special. The Country Cat uses chef-driven technique and skill to elevate whole animal, craft American cooking into a rarified space, while being completely unpretentious. The Sappingtons are connected to each other, their community, their ingredients, and their customers in a way that's just as invitingly uncommon as their establishment. After all, it's not often that a family restaurant where kids eat free on Sundays is helmed by a three-time James Beard Award semifinalist.

7937 Southeast Stark St.
503-408-1414, thecountrycat.net

Portland's one-of-a-kind wine bar and restaurant.

When *Wine Enthusiast Magazine* named the Willamette Valley its 2016 Wine Region of the Year, it was validation and a badge of honor for just about anybody and everybody associated with winemaking in the Portland area. From a broader view, it helped to solidify the city's reputation as a new culinary Mecca. Liquid assets are a large part of any cuisine scene, and wine is chief among them. A premier food city benefits greatly from being near a commensurately accomplished wine region, and vice versa. And while a number of restaurants in Portland tout a tightly focused wine list, and a number of wine bars provide elevated charcuterie or small-plate options, few, if any, establishments balance food and wine equally. Except the Oui Wine Bar & Restaurant.

When co-founders Kate Norris and Tom Monroe opened the Southeast Wine Collective in 2012, it was already more than your standard wine bar. It was an event space and full urban wine-making facility, providing a place for like-minded vintners to grow their businesses and perfect their craft. The multifaceted, 5,000-square-foot space was something unique, not just within the Southeast Division-Clinton neighborhood, but throughout the city. However, Norris and Monroe had no intentions of building a kitchen or serving food in their wine bar. But, prior to opening the urban winery, Norris had worked at a local catering company with a talented culinary school graduate, Althea Grey Potter. The two were fast friends, sharing a love of food, wine, laughter, and hard work. Potter offered to run a food program at the winery if they ever changed their minds. They eventually did.

Top: The cozy Oui Wine Bar.
Above left: Southeast Wine Collective co-founder Kate Norris, left, and Chef Althea Grey Potter.
Above right: One of Chef Potter's flavor-packed dinner offerings.
Photos courtesy of Carly Diaz.

Althea Grey Potter grew up with a love of good food. In this she was certainly helped along by her parents. After spending time in the Philippines, they settled in rural Maine for a time before landing in Massachusetts. Every year they planted and harvested a huge vegetable garden. They pickled, preserved, and fermented. They made their own bread as well as kombucha. They routinely made Chinese and Indian food from scratch. When a friend of Potter's who was living in Portland described what was happening in the City of Roses, Althea bought a one-way ticket and enrolled in culinary school. She worked around town at some reputable restaurants before she got the call from Norris and Monroe. It took a little time to convince wine bar guests that there was, in fact, real food being produced in the back. But a menu as good as theirs has a way of making its presence known. The food is wine-centric and whimsical, bringing Potter's bold, globally inspired flavors together with a love of seasonal produce and the bounty of the Pacific Northwest. The Oui Wine Bar & Restaurant is an exquisite representation of what can happen when food and wine are given equal time.

2425 Southeast 35th Place
503-208-2061
sewinecollective.com/oui-wine-bar-restaurant

"I want to continue to push the boundaries of what winery or wine bar food can be. When I started cooking food with a wine focus, I was terrified all the time of making the 'wrong' food to have with wine. I made the food I thought I should make instead of the food I make now, the food I want to make. The food I need to make. My cooking is influenced by my parents, by my travels, and by my curiosity about that world. I feel as though I am only just beginning to express myself truly through my cooking, and I can't wait to see where it goes."   —Chef Althea Grey Potter

One of countless perfect pairings at Oui. Courtesy of Carly Diaz.

A series of properties that are more than just eclectic brewpubs.

In 1983, brothers Brian and Mike McMenamin opened the Barley Mill on Hawthorne as a beer-centric bar. During that same time, the brothers, along with others in the craft brewing scene, had successfully lobbied the Oregon legislature to allow pubs that served food to also brew and serve beer onsite—perhaps one of the finest drafts of paper ever pushed across a desk. As a result, the brewpub revolution ignited, and the McMenamin brothers helped lead the charge. But for them, it was about more than great beer and food. Far more.

The McMenamins bought up historic buildings and properties that had outlasted their original purpose. Saved from the wrecking ball, each was transformed into something entirely new. A brewpub, restaurant, movie theater, hotel, distillery, winery, coffee roaster, cigar bar, pool hall, golf course, music venue, and in many cases, a number of the aforementioned at the same property. A McMenamins is like Disneyland for grownups. Each one is lovingly restored, nuanced, and heavy with ambience—existing as its own world within the McMenamins universe. And every McMenamins has a magnificent story to tell. Case in point, Ringlers Pub at the Crystal Ballroom. In the teens and '20s Montrose Ringler was the dance hall king of Portland. And the Crystal Ballroom, originally the Cotillion Hall, was the crown jewel of Ringler's empire. The third floor of the building sported a floating dance floor, all the rage back in the days of the Lindy and the Charleston. The very first female police officer in the country, Lola Baldwin, was put on the payroll in Portland, where she was charged with monitoring the city's "Social Hygiene"—seeing to it that young women didn't spiral out into a life

Left: Boon's Treasury.
Right: Bagdad Theater & Pub.
Photos courtesy of McMenamins/Kat Nyberg.

of sex crime via the dance floor. Baldwin and Ringler often butted heads throughout the years over the cultural viability of dance in modern society. That same hall would become the Fillmore of the Northwest in the 1960s and '70s, hosting the likes of James Brown and the Grateful Dead. Today, as a McMenamins, the ground floor of the building is a bar and restaurant. The third floor, the Crystal Ballroom, is still a popular live music venue. And the second floor is home to a brewery and a special events area, playfully named after Lola Baldwin, who is most assuredly spinning in her grave.

There are now fifty-five McMenamins locations in Oregon and Washington, with more on the way. Yet somehow, each one is special and an integrated part of its community. Perhaps above everything else that McMenamins properties do, they reflect and serve the communities they reside in. They are more than places to get food and drink; they are historic lines of fabric woven into the cultural tapestry of the Northwest.

mcmenamins.com

MOTHER'S BISTRO & BAR

A legendary brunch destination that has become a Portland institution.

Chef Lisa Schroeder excels at a great number of things, not the least of which is defying convention. In 1992, she had one foot in the corporate world and the other in catering. She also happened to be raising a daughter. Short on time but long on passion and creativity, Schroeder lamented that no restaurants specialized in "Mother Food": meals that took time and care, that enlivened the soul as well as the palate. That realization set in motion a journey that would eventually culminate in Mother's Bistro & Bar. It wasn't an easy or direct path, however.

Schroeder left her marketing career behind and enrolled at the Culinary Institute of America, where she set herself apart, graduating with honors and being selected as one of the Top Ten Student Chefs in America by *Food and Wine Magazine*. She didn't waste any time earning her chops, working at Lespinasse and Le Cirque in New York. Hungry for more, she went on a world tour of inspiration, visiting Morocco, Spain, Switzerland, and Italy—and landing apprenticeships in France at Roger Verge's Moulin des Mougins

Chef Schroeder also celebrates the cuisine of moms from around the world with the "Mother of the Month" (or "M.O.M.") menu. "The special mother is called the Mother of the Month (or M.O.M.™), and her photograph, story and menu take a prominent place at the beginning of Mother's menu. We choose a mother that allows us to take advantage of the seasonal availability of ingredients, such as a Greek mother in the summer months and a Polish mother in the winter months."

Left: Chef Lisa Schroeder.
Right: Dinner options at Mother's.

and at Mark Veyrat's L'Auberge de L'Eridan. The experience only solidified the driving culinary concept behind Mother's: that the best food anywhere in the world comes from the home. And that by applying the skills and techniques she had honed during the course of her education and travels, Schroeder could produce a restaurant experience unlike any other.

When she returned to the US she relocated to Portland, where she worked at another storied breakfast restaurant, Besaw's. She served as chef there until the time was right to strike out on her own. Finally, in 2000, Chef Schroeder opened Mother's Bistro & Bar in downtown Portland. It didn't take long for her to receive proof of concept, earning the "Restaurant of the Year" award from *Willamette Week*. Numerous accolades followed, along with throngs of locals as well as out of towners. Standing in line at Mother's for weekend brunch is a time-honored tradition in this city. Some wild smoked salmon hashes are worth waiting for. However, dinner typically comes with less of a wait and equally delectable options, including perhaps the finest chicken & dumplings, slow-cooked pot roast, or meatloaf found in any restaurant or home kitchen in the state.

212 Southwest Stark St.
503-464-1122
mothersbistro.com

One of the city's best and most creative
Korean restaurants feels like home.

When Han Oak chef/owner Peter Cho's wife, Sun Young Park, found an available but particularly unconventional space in Northeast Portland's Ocean Complex, they had the same reaction— "Perfect." Their version of perfection was an open area with a roll-up door and an inviting courtyard. Attached to it: an apartment that could serve as the family home. To some, that set up might sound pretty far away from perfect. But as with everything in life, it's about perspective. And if you're a top-tier chef looking to open your own restaurant while simultaneously nurturing a young family, and hoping to accomplish both tasks well, you're going to have to get a little unconventional.

Born in Korea, Cho was raised in Springfield, Oregon. After attending the University of Oregon, he moved to New York to live with his brother. He looked into the possibility of attending culinary school before ultimately deciding it was too expensive. So Cho just went to work. He walked into April Bloomfield's Michelin-starred Spotted Pig and asked her for a job. And in one quantum leap he went from "I think I'll pass on school" to "Let's get some world-class experience." He worked with Bloomfield for the next decade, also spending time at her second Michelin-starred project, the Breslin in New York's Ace Hotel. When his mother became ill, Cho and Park returned to Oregon, settling in Portland in 2015. After securing that perfect space, the two began running pop-up dinners, and things blossomed from there. Because of location, word of mouth, and the fact that it was open on Mondays, Han Oak, which opened officially in 2016, became a popular hang-out for some of the city's best culinary minds, as well as chefs from out of town. With a creative and constantly changing Korean menu that drew inspiration from

Top left: Mentaiko. Photo courtesy of Stephanie Yao.

Top right: Beef Ramen. Photo courtesy of Stephanie Yao.

Above left: All the fixin's. Photo courtesy of Kari Young.

Above right: Chef Cho and staff in the kitchen. Photo courtesy of Grace Rivera.

everywhere, Han Oak also found success with the rest of the city's food-loving crowd. As family and friends, including the couple's two young children, mill about between the backyard, restaurant, and the apartment, Han Oak feels like an elevated dining experience that's transpiring at a backyard BBQ. And that's more or less what's happening. It is truly unique, and according to Cho, something that could only happen in Portland. Which might be true. But you'll also need the right couple of people with the proper perspective to Vulcan mind-meld an unconventional space into the perfect work/life balance.

511 Northeast 24th Ave.
971-225-0032
hanoakpdx.com

Among Portland's oldest establishments and a long-standing staple for brunch or dinner, specializing in bona fide comfort food.

Since its early twentieth century origins, Besaw's has seen many iterations: soda fountain, twenty-four-hour diner, and destination brunch spot, among others. Its current owner, Cana Flug, has been at the helm since 2005. During her tenure, she has seen Besaw's grow from favorite neighborhood nook to nationally acclaimed restaurant. Still, it's an establishment that exudes Old Portland warmth—a family place where kids grow up and then bring their kids, who then bring their kids. One of the reasons families keep coming back is because the familial vibe carries through into the staff. The majority of the crew has worked together for five to ten years. And it's evident. However, beyond all the warm and fuzzy, the restaurant delivers culinarily. The executive chef is Dustin Clark, who originally worked with Flug at one of Portland's pioneer farm-to-table restaurants, Wildwood. Clark studied under Cory Schreiber, Wildwood founder and executive chef, and he eventually took over as executive chef when Schreiber left. But long before the accolades and the Travel Channel, Besaw's was a humble neighborhood establishment opened by two men with a dream.

As neighborhood development continued its inevitable progression through Northwest Portland, Besaw's was driven from its 112-year home in 2015. A new space was secured two blocks away, however, and in February 2016, Besaw's 2.0 flung its doors open wide to a comfort-starved public. The original neon sign made the trek to the new location, however.

Left: A light squash dish. Photo courtesy of Aaron Lee.

Right: An elevated breakfast burrito. Photo courtesy of Aaron Lee.

In 1903, George Besaw and Medric Liberty saw their dream of owning a beer parlor and gambling hall to fruition. At the time, Portland was seeing an influx of loggers, longshoremen, and their families. Loggers themselves, Besaw and Liberty received the generous help of Henry Weinhard, one of Portland's first brewers, to finance their vision. An immediate success, Besaw's reputation was bolstered by location, being conveniently situated en route to the 1905 Lewis & Clark Worldwide Exposition. The onset of Prohibition meant the end of the dream for Liberty, who sold his half of the business to Besaw. To keep things up and running, he introduced simple home cooking to the establishment.

After Prohibition was repealed, Besaw's was granted the first liquor license in the state of Oregon. The Besaw family became deft at the culinary art of offering hearty food and a memorable experience at a good value. The cafe quickly became the most popular meeting place amongst locals, with a reputation for stiff drinks, scrumptious meals, and lively conversation. Besaw's ethos remains a simple one: provide delicious, seasonal, and local food and drink, with genuine warmth of heart.

1545 Northwest 21st Ave.
503-228-2619
besaws.com

One of the nation's finest curators of craft chocolate and a celebration of the relatively young artisanal scene.

Aubrey Lindley met Jesse Manis in Seattle, where Manis was working at Fran's Chocolates. Perhaps due in part to a mutual appreciation for the product, the two would fall in love, marry, and develop a business plan to open a shop specializing in the burgeoning artisanal market. The pair had noticed that you could go to any fine dining restaurant and every other course on the menu had a story: where it was from, how it was treated, and why it was on the plate. Then dessert would arrive, and if chocolate was involved, it was almost an afterthought with no origin and a completely missed opportunity.

It might be hard to believe, but when compared to other exalted foodstuffs, the transformation of flavor-grade cacao into high-quality chocolate is in a relative state of infancy. Not that chocolatiers haven't been making ornate, cacao-based creations for centuries. There has just been a reliance on sugar to mask the bitterness of what most of the world has access to, commodity-grade cacao. Roughly 90 percent of the world's chocolate is derived from a product that is hearty and resistant to disease, but also somewhat acrid and lacking in nuance. The remaining 10 percent of flavor-grade cacao is an entirely different story. Just like wine, a terroir is associated with growing regions of cacao. And similarly to wine or even coffee, the way the product is treated—roasting, conching, refining, etc.—coaxes different flavor profiles and textures.

Portland became an attractive location to Aubrey and Jesse. Not just because the city's culture would invite an artisanal undertaking like a chocolate shop showcasing bean to bar makers, but because the city had more producers at the time than any other in America.

Above left: The shop's exterior.

Top right: Great afternoon starter kit.

Above right: The craft chocolate lovers paradise that is Cacao.

In 2006, they opened Cacao. Craft chocolate was a new and exciting market, but there were no real established standards. Consequently, they became one of the country's best gatekeepers for the consumer. Appreciated by connoisseurs as much for what they don't carry as what they do, the ever-morphing selection of curated chocolate is widely considered to be among the best collections found anywhere. The couple celebrates the world's best craft chocolate, which also happens to include Portland pioneers like Woodblock and Pitch Dark, but they are also known for their drinking chocolates, selections from regional chocolatiers, and expert staff. Despite all the excitement around chocolate's newly found recognition, Aubrey keeps things in perspective, stating, "We are happy to help open up the world of craft chocolate to people. We offer samples, insight, and education. But at the end of the day, it's still chocolate. And chocolate should be fun."

414 Southwest 13th Ave.
503-241-0656, cacaodrinkchocolate.com

GRAIN & GRISTLE/
OLD SALT MARKETPLACE

Source, cultivate, and butcher the best that's out there. Get it on a plate and let it shine.

Growing up in a Pennsylvania Dutch and German family in Northern Indiana, Ben Meyer's farm-to-table credentials are hard to match. Farmers on both sides, his family made most of their food by hand. "We raised hogs, slaughtered them, and made all of the meats we needed throughout the year. Krauts, pickles, and staples were all grown and processed on the farm. My great-grandmother, Georgia, controlled all of the canning and most of the cooking for the family. We were raised at her hip, learning the basics. She managed the family garden, and made sure everyone was fed." His culinary chops are solid as well, having worked in a number of topflight restaurants around the country. In Portland, he worked the opening line at Toro Bravo and co-founded Ned Ludd.

Marcus Hoover designed and built a number of the best kitchens in Portland. He was the kitchen designer for Rose's Restaurant Equipment for ten years. He then went on to earn a culinary degree and build Genie's Cafe. Alex Ganum is the founder and head brewer of Upright Brewing, one of the most renowned and well respected breweries in what might be the craft brew capital of America. In 2010, the three Portland powerhouses joined forces to design, build, and open Grain & Gristle, a restaurant that would take the pairing of food and beer to an elevated status. A place where people could get exceptional beer coupled with farm-direct food that was unpretentious and affordable. And they nailed it, but that was just the beginning.

Above left: Working the pass at Grain & Gristle.

Top right: Tending the fire at Old Salt.

Above right: Meat display at Old Salt.

With the idea of building a small food system—purchasing whole ingredients direct from the producers and turning them into the best interpretations year round—they sought a larger space. A bigger kitchen, the programs to handle 100 percent whole animals, a canning line, and the facility to accommodate it all. They would also need more avenues for marketing the meat. So they opened Old Salt Marketplace, sporting a full butcher shop, processing line, animal processing area, deli, and a Supperhouse. The cuisine is, as Meyer describes it, "truly American—borrowing from any technique or region, so long as we can do it well, and it accentuates the ingredient." Meats are cooked over an open hearth, vegetables are treated in the simplest way possible. The processed canned goods are used in-house as well as for retail and wholesale. They also serve a deli lunch all week long and are the proud owners of a butcher case that boasts some of the best and freshest meat in the city.

Grain & Gristle, 1473 Northeast Prescott St., 503-288-4740, grainandgristle.com

Old Salt Marketplace, 5027 Northeast 42nd Ave., 971-255-0167, oldsaltpdx.com

Serving Chinese-American classics since 1944.

It wasn't that long ago that Southeast 82nd Avenue was thought of as little more than a four-mile stretch of used-car dealerships, gas stations, and multifaceted illicit behavior. Over the last several years, things have started to shift, however, especially from a culinary standpoint. Historically, Portland has not been very ethnically diverse. And the official Chinatown on the west side of the river is a Chinatown in name only. The city's real epicenter for Asian cuisine now resides along Southeast 82nd. More than a Chinatown, the "Avenue of Roses," as it's referred to on the street signs, is also home to thriving Korean, Vietnamese, Thai, and Latino communities, with the majority of the markets, businesses, and restaurants reflecting that fact. But long before 82nd became the official hub for world cuisine in Portland, the Canton Grill helped lay the foundation for what the avenue would evolve into decades later.

In the 1920s and '30s, the building that houses the restaurant today was an open-fronted farmers market. Having acquired the property, Fred Louis Sr., Wayne Leong, and Eddie Louis converted it into a Chinese restaurant, the Canton Grill, which opened on August 29, 1944. Post–World War II, it became a dance hall hot spot. Folding tables and chairs were placed on the dance floor to accommodate the dinner rush. After 9 p.m., the tables were cleared and colored flood

The Canton Grill is also very much a family success story. Fred Louis Sr. passed the restaurant down to his son, Fred Louis Jr., who in turn has handed the business over to his daughters. Today, Cindy Louis serves as co-owner/general manager of the generationally beloved restaurant.

Left: Eddie Louis getting a hug.
Right: The extended Canton Grill family in the 1950s.

lights, mirror balls, and big band music kept patrons entertained late into the evening. Oregon law at the time mandated a BYOB approach, and guests would bring their own personally labeled liquor bottles.

Through the '50s and '60s, the restaurant stayed competitive by providing the family dinners and discounts that were the hallmark of the era. The Canton Grill doubled its seating capacity with the addition of the Dragon Room. As the '60s drew to a close, the Dragon Room became the Dragon Lounge, and the now well known life-sized Ho Ti good luck statue was put in place to greet guests. To this day, Ho Ti doubles as Santa Claus during the Christmas season. In the '70s, a grand piano was introduced into the Dragon Lounge, converting it into a sing-along piano bar. The '80s ushered in combo meals and additional parking. And in the '90s the owners increased the vegetarian options and introduced spicier Northern Chinese cuisine, to-go parking, and karaoke. The Canton Grill has stayed relevant by remaining true to its core values while also adapting to the changing times. It is an Old Portland restaurant that helped pave the way to the New Portland on Southeast 82nd Avenue.

2610 Southeast 82nd Ave.
503-774-1135
canton-grill.com

DAN & LOUIS OYSTER BAR

Celebrating the glories of the oyster for more than one hundred years in Portland's oldest family restaurant.

Louis C. Wachsmuth was born into an oyster-loving family in San Francisco in 1877. By 1881, the family had moved to Oysterville, Washington, where they cultivated the oyster beds of Shoalwater Bay for a living. When Wachsmuth's father retired, he moved to the big city of Portland to make a living. In 1904 he began working as a driver for the Oysterville Oyster Company, where he met his future wife, Lizzie Sauer. Then, in 1907, Wachsmuth and his business partner L. Roland Mills opened the City Oyster Company on Ankeny between 2nd and 3rd, specializing in oysters, crab, and fresh fish. Over the next two decades, Louis and Lizzie started a family as Mills moved on to other business ventures, leaving sole ownership to the Wachsmuths. The hot oyster stews and cocktails on the City Oyster Company menu were becoming increasingly popular, and the business expanded into an actual restaurant. Wachsmuth changed the restaurant's name to Louie's Oyster Bar and used City Oyster Company as the name for the oyster bed business he had recently acquired in Yaquina Bay. Newspaper men who frequented the

Some quotes have staying power. In 1930 when Louis C. Wachsmuth told a newspaper man, "Oyster soup is mighty nice. So is pepper roast and a fancy roast. A good many people prefer an oyster loaf. Others like an oyster pie. I have a book that gives 98 recipes for cooking an oyster. But as I've said before, I like them raw, and the best way of all is to eat 'em alive." He inadvertently gave the restaurant it's unofficial tagline, "Eat 'em alive."

Left: Oysters and Bloody Marys.

Right: Oysters: an Oregon commodity for well over a century.

restaurant coined the name "Dan & Louis Oyster Bar" because Wachsmuth's son, Dan, was always working side by side with his father. When Dan died of pneumonia at the age of twenty-seven, the name of the restaurant was officially changed as a memorial to his untimely death.

In 1957, Louis Wachsmuth passed on, leaving his family to continue the thriving restaurant and bar. He also left a legacy as one of the first advocates for clean water, leading the charge against ocean pollution. Dan & Louis Oyster Bar has continued to be passed down through generations in the Wachsmuth family. A restaurant business is inherently difficult to sustain, and in recent decades a combination of factors, including economic downturn and the changing face of the neighborhood that the restaurant has always called home, forced the business to the brink of extinction. But the current owner/operators, Keoni and Michelle Wachsmuth, have fought through the hard times. In a labor of familial love, they have brought Dan & Louis into the next era. The historic restaurant, decorated with more than a century's worth of nautical memorabilia, has also seen a boost in business thanks to the Ankeny Alley Association—the project that closed the street to automotive traffic and turned the once questionable thoroughfare into a well-lit, open-air seating area for business in the alley.

208 Southwest Ankeny St.
503-227-5906
danandlouis.com

A brewpub with an equal focus on beer and food.

If you enjoy craft beer, especially craft beer from Oregon, you have sampled the wares of John Harris. The 2018 Oregon Beer Hall of Fame inductee and owner/brewmaster of Portland's Ecliptic Brewing started his career at McMenamins. He then brewed at another Oregon icon, Deschutes, where he developed the recipes for some of the most well known and beloved beers in the craft beer world to this day—including Obsidian Stout, Mirror Pond Pale Ale, Jubelale, and Black Butte Porter. Next, he moved on to a twenty-year career at Hood River's Full Sail Brewery, creating the Brewmaster Reserve line. In 2013, John finally opened his own brewpub, Ecliptic, as an homage to his love of brewing and astronomy. But there would be another focus as well. Food. To elevate the food menu to the same level as the beer list, Harris brought in Executive Chef Michael Molitor.

Molitor had worked in restaurants in Boise, Idaho, chipping away at a political science degree. While working at a popular Italian restaurant, he developed a love for cooking and discovered the love of his life, a server named Greta, whom he would marry and start a family with. Molitor eventually took on the role of sous chef at one of the best new restaurants in town, and the education in political science was replaced with a culinary one. After culinary school, the young couple moved to Portland, where Molitor took on an externship at the Heathman before assuming the role of sous chef at the Hotel Vintage Plaza's Pazzo Ristorante for nine years. Then, in 2013, he teamed up with Harris to become the executive chef at Ecliptic.

Molitor's challenge was to create a menu that complemented the beer, but which could also stand on its own merits. He wanted to accomplish two things—satisfy classic brewpub expectations and provide seasonal, unexpected rotating choices. The plan came together

Top left: John Harris.

Top right: The seasonal Goat Mole Tacos with beer pairing.

Above: Patio seating at Ecliptic.

nicely, with every seasonal item on the menu having a suggested beer pairing. In accordance with the ecliptic, the earth's yearly path around the sun, the beer and food menus change every six weeks on the old-world calendar: Samhain, Winter Solstice, Brighid, Spring Equinox, Beltaine, Summer Solstice, Lammas, and the Autumnal Equinox. Ecliptic Brewing has proven itself to be the "missing link" in the evolution of beer and food. Bringing together the seasonality, creativity, and craft of both, it is a new species that pushes boundaries and sets a higher bar for what a brewpub can be.

825 North Cook St.

503-265-8002

eclipticbrewing.com

Elevated vegan cuisine, presented in an entertaining and informative tasting menu format.

Growing up as a latchkey kid, Aaron Adams learned how to cook for himself. He was by no means a neglected child, finding extensive comfort in the Cuban family meals that provide him with fond memories to this day. But the time spent alone after school with Public Broadcasting System cooking shows sparked something, as he developed a penchant for throwing dinner parties for his friends. He would bounce around a bit before attending culinary school in Miami and opening his first restaurant in Jacksonville, Florida.

Chef Adams's development as a chef was both personal and professional. He had a great affinity for French cuisine and fine dining, but he wasn't the biggest fan of the exclusivity that often came with them. At the same time, his own health wasn't where he wanted it to be. He was smoking, drinking, and putting on more than a few extra pounds. Something had to change, and his body and culinary ethos began morphing simultaneously.

Foie gras was the first to go, and the beef became exclusively grass-fed before leaving his menus entirely. He landed in Portland, and after working a number of other gigs, he founded the vegan restaurant Farm Spirit to be the culmination of a man urged forward by uncompromising ethics, increased focus on health, and sharp culinary talent. As you might expect, the restaurant sources from a

Dispelling some misconceptions about veganism, Chef Adams is also a prolific powerlifter–opening his own gym, Strength Union, in early 2018. Proving that animal protein and strength don't necessarily go hand in hand.

A sampling of an eighteen-course dinner service. Photo courtesy of Nikki Unger Fink.

number of local farms, artisans, and purveyors—people and places Adams has strong relationships with. In the end, his approach and philosophy helped produce the best representation of what Chef Adams calls the "horticultural cuisine of Cascadia." He wryly admits it is the most pretentious way to describe what the restaurant does, but it is an apt description.

Beyond that, Farm Spirit delivers on Chef Adams's desire to provide his guests with an elevated, entertaining, and memorable experience. Seated along the open chef's counter, patrons are treated to a ringside view of the chef and his team as they prepare and describe each course in real time. A dinner service is typically comprised of six to eight main courses, bolstered by a number of smaller plates and bites for a total of thirteen to fifteen courses. It isn't "replacement" cuisine, utilizing meat-like imitation dishes. The vegetables are the star of each dish, focusing on what they contribute and not what they don't. The plates are elegant, beautiful, and, most importantly, delicious. Chef Adams is producing local and seasonal vegan fare, executed and presented with a casual, fine-dining flare.

1414 Southeast Morrison St.
farmspiritpdx.com

Portland's oldest restaurant continues to thrive, almost 140 years after it first opened its doors.

In 1879 Louis Eppinger opened the Bureau Saloon in Portland. A young barkeep named Frank Huber would become part owner of the business before buying the saloon outright from Eppinger and changing the name to Huber's in 1895. Prior to the name change, Huber hired a young immigrant from Canton, China, as a cook. It was 1891, and Louie Way Fung, aka Jim Louie, was fourteen— having stowed away on a clipper ship in hopes of a better life in America. Huber, ever the forward thinker, had the idea of offering a free turkey sandwich with every alcoholic beverage purchased. He didn't know it at the time, but that little gesture would morph into a time-honored tradition. In 1910, the saloon moved into its current location on 3rd Avenue. When Frank Huber passed away in 1911, he left Huber's to his wife, Augusta. Having little knowledge of the saloon business, she turned over the day-to-day operations to Jim Louie.

At the onset of Prohibition, Louie transitioned the establishment into a restaurant with a focus on roast turkey dinners, something he had a particularly good handle on. In addition to an expanded menu of food offerings, Huber's provided something else that brought a steady stream of customers through the door—"Special Tea." Or, for those unfamiliar with the code-laden parlance of the Prohibition era, Canadian Whiskey. In 1940, Augusta Huber passed away, leaving the

One of the best shows in Portland is the production of the Spanish Coffee at Huber's. It is a spectacle, as if Cirque du Soleil and a bartender had a baby. It's also delicious.

Left: The historic bar area at Huber's.
Right: Louie Way Fung, aka Jim Louie.

business to her son, John, who sold half the business to Jim Louie for the sum of one dollar. It wasn't long before Louie's health began to fade, and he passed his share of the business to the only person he could, his nephew, Andrew. Because of the Chinese Exclusion Act, Jim's wife and children were not allowed to come to America. But because Andrew was born in Portland, he had citizenship and could legally take on the business. In 1952, Andrew bought out John Huber to become the sole proprietor. Andrew and his wife, Amy, dutifully ran the restaurant for a remarkable stretch of almost four decades, from 1946 until 1987. Andrew passed in 1989, followed closely by Amy in 1990. They willed the business to their daughter, Lucille, along with her sons, James and David—the two gentlemen who currently run it.

In an era of hyper-seasonality, Instagrammable plating, and self-bussing, Huber's stands out of time and place, in the best possible way. It's dark wood and class, service and civility. And the bar, which is on the National Register of Historic Places, remains almost completely intact from 1910. With its stained-glass skylight, mahogany paneling, Gothic arches, and terrazzo floor, it's one of the finest dining rooms here or anywhere. Very little has changed over the course of the last half century at Huber's. But that's because almost nothing has had to.

411 Southwest 3rd Ave.
503-228-5686
hubers.com

One of Portland's most visited tourist destinations.

When co-owners Kenneth "Cat Daddy" Pogson and Tres Shannon opened Voodoo Doughnut in 2003, they had no way of knowing how enormously popular the Old Town doughnut shop would become. It's quite possible that centuries from now, cultural anthropologists will point towards the purveyors of the iconically irreverent pastries as the men who spawned an era. The friends were already well known entities in the Portland music and bar scene when they shook hands to go into business together. After assessing the landscape and determining that the gritty neighborhood they worked in was void of doughnuts, the business plan wrote itself. They pulled some strings and got access to the old Berbati's kitchen at the corner of Southwest 3rd and Ankeny. In an area of town hallmarked by homeless shelters and dive bars, the duo opened a doughnut shop that proved to be an instant hit with the area's eclectic clientele.

The ever-expanding lineup of unique doughnuts included offerings topped with breakfast cereal, Tang, bacon, and for a very brief, FDA-abbreviated amount of time, Nyquil and Pepto Bismol. Over the next decade, Voodoo Doughnut became so popular that the iconic pink boxes are still ubiquitous fixtures in the hands of tourists walking around town or lining up for homeward bound airplanes at PDX. And as world domination moves forward, there are now locations in Eugene, Denver, Austin, Hollywood, and Orlando.

22 Southwest 3rd Ave.
503-241-4704
voodoodoughnut.com

Top: Inside Voodoo Doughnut. Photo courtesy of Rockobilly.

Above left: The Butterfinger Doughnut. Photo courtesy of Shawnalee Anderton.

Above right: The legendary Bacon Maple Bar. Photo courtesy of Shawnalee Anderton.

CHAMELEON RESTAURANT & BAR

One of the most unique eateries in Portland recently celebrated its twentieth anniversary.

Pat Jeung grew up in Laos near the Thai border. To call it a tumultuous upbringing would be an understatement. After the Vietnam War, his family routinely hid from roving militia groups. A bullet even once grazed his brother's hair. Things were not as stressful in the family kitchen, however. Jeung was raised in a gender-blind family. Everybody in the household was expected to cook—an unusual upbringing for the time and place that would serve him well in later life.

Jeung, at the age of sixteen and along with his brothers and sisters, received refugee status and moved to Portland. While still in high school and taking English classes at night, he got a job at McDonald's. Work ethic, outgoingness, and maturity were traits Jeung already had in spades, and as his English improved, he quickly rose to shift manager. He'd routinely clock out around 2:30 a.m., catch a few hours of sleep, and then trek back off to school. Lather, rinse, repeat.

After high school, Jeung moved to Los Angeles before returning to Portland at twenty-two. Having gained kitchen experience in L.A., he opened his own restaurant, Thai Cuisine, in the late '80s. When it closed in 1993, Jeung promised himself that the next restaurant would focus entirely on his style of cooking, which includes some significant world influence. Jeung is a dedicated traveler, having covered Asia, Europe, South America, and China. But he doesn't do it the way most of us do. He ingratiates himself into a culture and sets up work stints at regional restaurants. He'll stay in a place for

Left: Garden dining at Chameleon.

Right: Pat Jeung, middle, learning from chefs in Tuscany, Italy.

weeks or months, soaking up the culture and cuisine like a sponge before reimagining and incorporating what he's learned into his own cuisine—Jeung fusion. Keeping his promise to himself, in 1997 Jeung opened the Chameleon Restaurant & Bar, offering dishes like Italian meatballs with lemongrass and Thai chilies, as well as duck ravioli in red curry. It's that sort of menu that loyal patrons have come to expect. Jeung stays up on what's happening around him culinarily, but he pays no mind to what's trendy. He changes the menu when he feels inspired to do so, sourcing much of the produce from his own garden. The restaurant itself is as unique as Jeung's cuisine, boasting chandeliers, a grand piano, and an extensive, two-hundred-seat patio. Twenty years later, it looks like the decision to do his own thing has paid off.

2000 Northeast 40th Ave.
503-460-2682
chameleonpdx.co

Gloriously upholding the tradition of American tiki bars.

Broadway is the thoroughfare that runs through the heart of downtown Portland. If you continue north, the street crosses the Willamette River and becomes Northeast Broadway. The change goes beyond nomenclature, however. The area between Lloyd Center and the popular Hollywood neighborhood is mostly commercial—some restaurants, bars, grocery stores, and nail salons. Set in the midst of a particularly nondescript row of businesses is an establishment that is anything but. Camouflaged in plain sight, Hale Pale was named the third best tiki bar in the world in 2017 by tiki bar authority Critiki—the second year in a row it has earned that distinction. That's not a total surprise, however. Martin Cate knows his tiki bars. The owner and creator of the world-famous Smuggler's Cove in San Francisco, Cate brought his expert knowledge of cocktails and tiki culture to Portland in 2012.

Entering the bar, patrons pass over a small "bridge" into the main space and are instantly surrounded by multicolored lights, puffer fish,

"I like to say that although any time you visit a bar you are looking for escape, tiki offers the ultimate escape. The lights, sounds, smells, elaborately decorated and mysteriously flavored cocktails surround you and transport you outside of the day-to-day monotony. A conversation I had a few months ago made me realize it goes even deeper than that–there's something related to the comfort and safety of childhood that is recaptured in the best tiki experiences; we're not just escaping from something, we're actually escaping to something."
–Paddy Holland, General Manager, Hale Pele

A lineup of cocktails.

tiki carvings, statues, and various island décor. Every hour there's a simulated thunderstorm, as well as a volcano that erupts whenever a group orders a "volcano bowl" to share. Hale Pele—"House of the Volcano Goddess"—pays dutiful homage to what's best about America's love affair with tiki. Classic and contemporary exotic cocktails are made with fresh juices, premium spirits, and house-made syrups. It's a robust and remarkable lineup of drink options. And for rum fans, the Hale Pele collection encompasses more than 300 rums from around the world. The food menu is mainly Hawaiian/Polynesian and Asian inspired. It's also quite impressive given that the true focus of the bar is, well, the bar. Hale Pele is not a large establishment. It's cozy and filled with thoughtful details that could take a frequent visitor months or years to catalog. Trust me on that one. Yet it somehow plays larger. Even when it's filled to capacity, which is frequently, the bar never feels claustrophobic, rather convivial and celebratory. It's a true tiki bar, and Portland is thankful to have it. Trust me on that one, too.

2733 Northeast Broadway
503-662-8454, halepele.com

A Roman-inspired Italian restaurant and one of the city's most coveted dinner spots.

It's not often that a restaurant comes out of the gate hot and stays that way, years after its debut. But that's exactly what happened with Ava Gene's. Duane Sorensen, of Stumptown Coffee and the Woodsman Tavern fame, opened Ava Gene's with Executive Chef Joshua McFadden driving the menu. And McFadden drove it hard. After attending Portland's Le Cordon Bleu, he worked in renowned kitchens on both coasts, including San Francisco's Lark Creek Inn and Momofuku in New York. But it was his time spent managing Eliot Coleman's Four Season Farm in Maine that helped define his culinary ethos. According to McFadden, "It was the culmination of my thinking about fruits, vegetables, and seasonality. Ava Gene's was created from the idea of drawing on the best of what the Northwest has to offer in order to create a local, seasonal take on Roman cuisine."

That they did. The aggressively seasonal menu relies heavily on strong relationships with area farmers and ranchers. McFadden's love of vegetables is evident in all plates and in all seasons. His deft hand extends into the restaurant's pastas, which are made from regional grains, hand-rolled, and house-extruded. A regional Italian wine list accentuates the cuisine. In accordance, *Wine Enthusiast* has

> "Our restaurants will always be defined by their relationship to local farmers, ranchers, and purveyors . . . from the radish in the salad to the soap in the bathroom. Diners can come experience those things knowing that the service will create an environment that is fun, comfortable, and caring."
> –Executive Chef Joshua McFadden

Left: An assortment of seasonal offerings. Photo courtesy of A. J. Meeker.

Right: Dinner, family-style. Photo courtesy of A. J. Meeker.

named Ava Gene's one of America's 100 Best Wine Restaurants every year since opening in 2013. A creative cocktail menu and extensive selection of amari and grappa only add to the restaurant's list of lauded liquid assets. And *Bon Appétit* magazine named it the #5 Best New Restaurant in America shortly after opening. In 2016, McFadden and business partner Luke Dirks negotiated the sale of Ava Gene's to Submarine Hospitality, which then opened one of the city's favorite new restaurants, Tusk. And the hits keep on coming. Since opening, Ava Gene's has been featured in *Condé Nast Traveler*, the *New York Times, Food & Wine, Sunset*, and the *Wall Street Journal*. In 2017, McFadden's debut cookbook, *Six Seasons: A New Way with Vegetables*, was released to acclaim and named a Best Cookbook of the Year by the *Wall Street Journal*, the *Atlantic, Bon Appetit, Food Network Magazine, Every Day with Rachael Ray, USA Today*, the *Seattle Times, Eater*, and more. But despite McFadden's well-earned reputation for elevated and inspired, fans of traditional Italian dishes need not worry. The menu features a rotating selection of classic nightly specials, like sugo on Sunday, meatballs on Monday, and a fish fry on Friday.

3377 Southeast Division St.

971-229-0571

avagenes.com

The seminal French restaurant every city needs.

Culinary influence varies greatly from childhood to childhood. And all things considered, Chef Aaron Barnett's youth was pretty good. Born to Scottish lineage in Alberta, Canada, Barnett's family spent time in Manitoba before moving to Los Angeles. His parents were foodies who loved to cook. His father in particular had a penchant for old-school French food, making demi-glace from scratch and sauces that took days to produce. Los Angeles inspired the whole family. A world of influence opened up, including Vietnamese, Indian, and Mexican flavor profiles. Barnett remembers coming home from school to find his mother making ceviche or Peking duck. She would also occasionally quiz him on what he was eating— what flavors was he getting from the dish? Pretty heady stuff for a fourth grader, but itwould serve him well in the future.

Post high school, Barnett performed a familiar dance of indecision—finish college? Veterinary school? Culinary school it is. After attending the California School of Culinary Arts' Cordon Bleu program, he externed at Lumière in Vancouver, British Columbia, where he discovered a new influence, the fresh flavors of the Northwest. He went on to work in San Francisco and even take an executive chef position in Palm Springs. By this time, his best friend from school had settled in Portland, and Barnett would take an occasional restaurant-themed trip to the Northwest. The scene was electric, with many restaurants that would later become cornerstones just finding their legs. With the availability of exceptional produce and a significantly more affordable cost of living sweetening the pot, moving to Portland became an obvious choice.

After working at a few different restaurants around town, he found a cozy spot on Southeast Clinton, the birthplace of the original St.

Left: Chef Aaron Barnett.
Right: The open kitchen at St. Jack.

Jack. Chef Barnett's modern take on a Lyonnais bouchon, St. Jack is driven by technique and flavor profiles. Hearty, rich, and rustic: bone marrow, butter, pigs' heads, sweet breads, foie gras. Some dishes take days to produce. The restaurant is constantly evolving, however, with one foot in the past and one in the future. The move of St. Jack to Northwest 23rd saw the introduction of higher-end fare. For balance, Barnett opened La Moule back on Southeast Clinton to maintain a more casual and accessible option. Regardless of what he's serving or where, you can be sure that the flavors will be right. His parents saw to that.

St. Jack
1610 Northwest 23rd Ave.
503-360-1281
stjackpdx.com

La Moule
2500 Southeast Clinton St.
971-339-2822
lamoulepdx.com

ST. HONORÉ BOULANGERIE

A standout in a city riddled with top-tier bakeries.

Few if any individuals making breads or pastries in Portland possess the pedigree of St. Honoré Boulangerie owner and master baker Dominique Geulin. Hailing from the small Normandy town of Etretat, Geulin learned the art of baking from his father in the family bakery they lived above. After high school, he enrolled in The Baking School, in nearby Rouen. In the early '80s he was invited to come to Portland to help open Le Panier, an authentic French bakery in Old Town. Five years later Geulin left Portland to bake and train abroad, but the City of Roses left an impression. In 1990, while waiting for a work permit to return to Portland, he entered France's most prestigious competition and received the award of Meilleur Ouvrier de France, the esteemed MOF, in the boulangerie category from late French president François Mitterand. Dominique returned to Portland the following year and opened St. Honoré Boulangerie in December 2003, the first of four locations.

The oven used at St. Honoré is a clay firebrick bread oven common in traditional French baking. The bricks are made from the kaolin earth of the town of Larnage, located in the foothills of the Rhone Valley. The quarries there have been in use since

> In May 2016, the French National Minister of Agriculture selected Dominique to receive the status of Chevalier (Knight) in the Order of Agricultural Merit. This order of merit was established in 1883 to recognize distinguished service in the area of agriculture.

Above left: Geulin making his Galette des Rois pastry.

Top right: Enjoying a light lunch at the counter, while baking continues. Photo courtesy of Adam Sawyer.

Above right: The traditional clay firebrick oven.

Roman times. The clay's refractory properties have a natural moisture retention that transfers the heat evenly, working some serious old-world magic on whatever you decide to stick into one of those things. And in the case of St. Honoré, that includes soups, sandwiches, and savory entrees.

2335 Northwest Thurman St. (Original Location)
503-445-4342
sainthonorebakery.com

Exquisite architecture and tea/food pairings in one of the city's most serene and beautiful settings.

As if any of us needed another reason to visit the Japanese Garden. One of Portland's crown jewels, the garden possesses an alluring tranquility that captivates in all seasons. But after a recent renovation that includes the addition of the Umami Cafe, your increased frequency of visitation will be justifiable. Renowned Japanese architect Kengo Kuma, described by many as the Frank Lloyd Wright of Japan, has transformed the entire area above the parking lot into a Cultural Village with the floating, cantilevered Umami Cafe hanging over the hill path.

The design is reminiscent of Kyoto's Kiyomizu-dera temple and provides wide open views of the garden's entrance and the hillside below. The Tokyo-based Jugetsudo tea company provides tea alongside light, exquisitely paired snacks from Japanese food company Ajinomoto, as well as several local Japanese confectioneries. In addition, visitors to the cafe will be treated to *omotenashi*—great attention to service. The staff at the cafe are trained in proper Japanese tea preparation and service. The Umami Cafe could stand on its own as a destination. But having the Japanese Garden for a backyard does not hurt at all.

611 Southwest Kingston Ave.
503-223-1321
japanesegarden.org/umami-cafe

Top: A selection of tea/food pairings.

Above left: The exterior of the Umami Cafe. Photo courtesy of Bruce Forster.

Above right: The cafe's interior. Photo courtesy of Bruce Forster.

SIGNAL STATION PIZZA

A more unique eatery in Portland than this old gas station turned neighborhood pizzeria may not exist.

St. Johns was its own town until Portland annexed it in 1915. The downtown or Main Street area still holds a Mayberry-esque charm, punctuated by one of the first buildings encountered upon entering the neighborhood—Signal Station Pizza. Originally a gas station when it was built in the 1930s, it has had a few different incarnations since then, including a flower shop. It's been a neighborhood pizzeria for decades now, but a pair of lovingly restored gas pumps and neon lighting keep the memory of the building's original intent alive. While not designed with the notion of housing a large pizza oven so much as an even larger Lincoln or Cadillac, the kitchen is cozy and efficient. The staff hand-makes the dough, sauces, and most everything else that can be produced in house. It is a damn fine slice of pie. And if you're able to combine it with a pint of Bridgeport IPA on a Northwest summer evening when the neon glow perfectly matches the sunset, the true meaning of the phrase "happy hour" will be quite evident.

8302 North Lombard St.
503-286-2257
signalstationpizza.com

The building, which appears on the National Register of Historic Places, has long been a favorite among photographers, as demonstrated by its appearance in countless classic-car photo shoots and even the occasional television spot.

Above left: The exterior of Signal Station Pizza. Photo courtesy of Adam Sawyer.

Top right: The St. Johns Combo. Photo courtesy of Adam Sawyer.

Above right: The Chopped Salad. Photo courtesy of Adam Sawyer.

Portland's understanding of regional Thai cuisine, expanded.

Born and raised in Bangkok, Thailand, Akkapong "Earl" Ninsom grew up in the kitchen. When he was eight years old, his mother got sick and he cooked his first meal to make her feel better. During summers, he would visit a grandparent in Surat Thani, where he learned to cook Southern Thai food. Visits to a grandmother in the Lopburi Province introduced him to Central Thai–style cooking. As an adult, Ninsom moved to Los Angeles to work at his cousin's restaurant. While the experience was helpful, he didn't care much for L.A. Heeding the call of higher education and corporate security, Ninsom returned to Thailand and went on to graduate with a business degree and attend graduate school at one of Thailand's top universities, studying international economics. In his role as a senior merchandiser, he traveled throughout Southeast Asia and France. He caught the food bug again, and this time there was no cure.

When his family came to Portland, he followed. Ninsom cooked around town and helped various family members with their own culinary endeavors before striking out on his own in 2008. His restaurant succeeded, but he burned himself out. It also wasn't the same food that stirred his soul back in Thailand. He went to the drawing board and opened PaaDee in 2011. The new restaurant was closer to his style of cuisine, expanding the boundaries of what Portland considered to be Thai food. And they liked it. Then he was hired to cook for a private dinner party. He was given carte blanche to do what he wanted, which he did. To Ninsom's surprise, guests were enamored with the flavor profiles that heretofore had never graced their palates. Encouraged, he went full monty, opening Langbaan in 2016, along with world-class co-chef

Left: One of the ever-rotating regional offerings at Langbaan.
Right: Dinner service at Langbaan.

Rassamee Ruaysuntia, in the back room of PaaDee. The regional, unapologetically Thai-tasting menu surprised everybody—guests at what genuine Thai cuisine could be, and Ninsom himself at Portlanders loved of what genuine Thai cuisine could be. In a very short time, Langbaan went from "let's see how this works" to "perhaps the best Thai restaurant in America." The Midas touch hasn't left Ninsom's keep, either. In addition to PaaDee and Langbaan, he is currently a chef-owner of Hat Yai in Northeast, specializing in Southern Thai fried chicken, and a partner at the Kim Jong Smokehouse.

PaaDee/Langbaan
6 Southeast 28th Ave.
971-344-2564
langbaanpdx.com

Hat Yai
1605 Northeast Killingsworth St.
503-764-9701
hatyaipdx.com

Kim Jong Smokehouse
413 Northwest 21st Ave.
971-373-8990
kimjongsmokehouse.com

PORTLAND FARMERS MARKET AT PSU

Farm-to-table would be nothing without farms and the markets they supply. Countless growers in the Willamette Valley produce more than 240 different crops. The valley's bounty is the genesis of Portland's culinary movement. But beyond the valley to the south, the city's proximity to the Pacific Ocean out west and the ranches of the east help stock Portland's farmers markets to the gills. Augmented by culinary artisans and specialty food producers, the city of Portland is home to no fewer than twenty such markets. Chief among them is the nonprofit Portland Farmers Markets (PFM), with the headliner at the PSU Campus.

In 1992, three local activists—Craig Mosbaek, Ted Snider, and Dr. Richard Hagan—established the Portland Farmers Market with thirteen vendors in a parking lot at Albers Mill. The market grew and relocated to its current location at PSU in 1998, with a second location added at Shemanski Park. Things did not slow down. Over the years additional markets, including the Pearl, Pioneer Courthouse Square, Kenton, and the Lents International Farmers Market, were all opened or taken in under the PFM umbrella. Today, the year-round flagship market at PSU is home to more than two hundred vendors including farms, nurseries, bakeries, meat and

It is common to see restaurant chefs combing the market and snatching up what will become that evening's or the next day's menu offerings. Maya Lovelace, chef at Portland's Mae restaurant, is known for making excellent use of the Veggie Valet service offered by the market. A volunteer gathers and guards your produce until you're ready to tab up.

Top: Customers perusing the goods. Photo courtesy of Dave Adamshick.

Above left: The colors of the Portland Farmers Market. Photo courtesy of Dave Adamshick.

Above right: More than two hundred vendors to choose from. Photo courtesy of Dave Adamshick.

seafood providers, cheese makers, and more. During the height of the season, up to twenty thousand customers shop at the market each Saturday. Chef demonstrations, market music, and a lineup of food education events only add to the market's allure. Staff and volunteers at a yellow-tented information booth answer questions and provide direction.

1831 Southwest Pedestrian Trail
503-241-0032
portlandfarmersmarket.org/our-markets/psu

Authentic Israeli flavors in a vegan restaurant.

Tal Caspi is no stranger to exotic flavors and wide-reaching culinary influences. His family had moved from the Ukraine to Argentina before settling for a time in Israel, where his parents owned and operated a pizza restaurant. When he was just three, they moved to the United States, eventually settling in Los Angeles. Food was already a big part of Caspi's life, and his time spent in the culinary melting pot of L.A. did nothing to change that. At fourteen he moved back to Israel, where he absorbed the region's cuisine like a sponge. Years later Caspi made his way back to the states, landing work at a goat dairy in New Mexico. Despite having no formal culinary training, he was responsible for making every meal for everyone. This would be his career.

In 2006 he moved to Portland sight unseen. Like a number of other chefs new to town, he would feel out and find a way into the scene via food carts. After working for some other owners, including a stint at the legendary woodfired pizza cart Pyro Pizza, he opened his own cart, Gonzo. Specializing in Israeli street food, something Portland was all but void of, the cart earned fans quickly. As things progressed, Caspi moved the already vegetable-forward cuisine all the way to a vegan pop-up restaurant called Aviv. In 2017, he partnered with Sanjay Chandrasekaran, the owner of Portland's

Caspi has big plans for his brand, hoping to expand the restaurant up and down the West Coast. The roots are already spreading via his Gonzo packaged hummus and catering company.

Above left: Colorful Israeli fare at Aviv.

Top right: Flavorful hummus and cocktails.

Above right: The dining room at Aviv.

renown vegan Indian food restaurant, the Sudra, to open a brick and mortar version of the pop-up on Southeast Division.

In less than a year, Aviv has ensconced itself firmly into a burgeoning pack of vegan and vegetarian restaurants that are taking meatless cuisine to a new level in Portland. Everything is scratch made, including a remarkable lineup of flavored hummus and house-made rolls and pita bread. Aviv's flavors are bold and balanced and at times, almost scarily creative. For example—on paper, the Hatch Green Chile ice cream looks like it shouldn't exist. In reality, it very much needs to. Meat lovers have had it good in this town for quite some time. Thankfully, places like Aviv are helping to put a shine on the other side of the culinary coin.

1125 Southeast Division St.
503-206-6280
avivpdx.com

Insanely delicious food cart becomes a brick and mortar success story.

Let's say you're a chef and would like to open your own restaurant, but maybe you don't have the extra million dollars lying around the house to do so. Or perhaps you're new in town and you want to get a feel for the landscape or demonstrate proof of concept before sinking your life savings into a project. In Portland, you've got options. Namely, food carts. A great case in point is Rick Gencarelli. Growing up in Connecticut, a young Gencarelli got a job as a busboy and never looked back.

In 1992, he enrolled at the Culinary Institute of America in New York. Gencarelli worked an externship at Aqua in San Francisco, followed by four years as sous chef at Todd English's Olives in Boston. After heading back to the West Coast, he worked at both Rubicon and One Market restaurants in San Francisco. Back to the East Coast once more, he opened Miramar Restaurant in Westport, Connecticut, then two years later, Olives Restaurant in the W Hotel in New York City. Not one to grow roots, Gencarelli and his family left for Vermont three years after that, where he became the chef at the Inn at Shelburne Farms on Lake Champlain.

In 2009, as was the case for many chefs, the lure of Portland's food scene was too strong, and Chef Gencarelli made one more move. Discovering food carts through his wife's recommendations, he decided that a cart would be the best way to get his name in the community and showcase his talents without making a major leap of faith. He opened the Lardo food cart in September 2010, serving wildly creative, progressive, and flavorful sandwiches anchored by old-world techniques. Lardo itself is a salume made by curing strips of fatback with rosemary and other herbs and spices. Gencarelli had an inkling that savory, pork-based sandwiches would be a hit, and a

Left: The Pork Meatball Banh Mi. Photo courtesy of Alan Weiner Photography.
Center: Chef/Owner Rick Gencarelli. Photo courtesy of Alan Weiner Photography.
Right: The Pho-rench Dip Sandwich. Photo courtesy of Alan Weiner Photography.

great introduction to the people of Portland. His Porchetta sandwich, featuring roast pork on ciabatta with hazelnut gremolata and lemon-caper aioli, was an instant hit and a fine how-do-you-do to a swine-loving city. Two years later, he opened the first brick and mortar location on Southeast Hawthorne, followed by a second location in Southwest that shares space with his second restaurant offering, Grassa. This handcrafted counter service pasta restaurant was another instant hit that soon earned a second location as well. It's quite possible that Chef Gencarelli would have won over the hearts and stomachs of Portland had he gone straight into a restaurant, but that cart-based handshake he chose to offer the city first certainly didn't hurt anything.

Lardo
1212 Southeast Hawthorne Blvd.
503-234-7786

1205 Southwest Washington St.
503-241-2490
lardosandwiches.com

Grassa
1205 Southwest Washington St.
503-241-1133

1506 Northwest 23rd Ave.
971-386-2916
grassapdx.com

Elevated, regional American fare with a Midwest accent.

Sarah Pederson was raised in Wisconsin. True to her roots, she has a strong affinity for beer, soul-satisfying comfort food, and the Green Bay Packers. If you weigh all of those factors, North Portland's Saraveza—the combination of her name and the Spanish word for beer, *cerveza*—makes perfect sense. But her route to becoming the owner of Portland's favorite beer bar/restaurant was a bit more circuitous than you might expect. After attending college, Pederson landed in Los Angeles, where she got into music public relations. It wasn't where her heart was, but it paid the bills. When she received a raise and promotion, Pederson became almost physically ill at the thought of an unfulfilling life path being laid out before her, so she quit.

After hearing friends describe Portland, she moved to the City of Roses and fell in love with the beer scene. She went to school to become a brewer, only to discover that the brewing process wasn't her true calling, either. In helping a friend run one of the city's favorite dessert spots, Pix Patisserie, she discovered that she truly enjoyed customer service. It dawned on Pederson that noplace in Portland was offering what she wanted—a cozy place where the food was good and the beer and beer education were great. So she went home to write a business plan, and in 2008 she opened Saraveza. Since then, Portlanders who love great beer, food, and/or an inviting place to watch the Green Bay Packers couldn't be happier.

1004 North Killingsworth St.
503-206-4252
saraveza.com

Left: The gameday favorite, fried cheese curds.

Right: The Saraveza beer cooler.

HAIR OF THE DOG BREWING COMPANY

One of the first brewpubs in Portland, and still one of the most inventive and beloved.

Alan Sprints moved to Portland in 1988 to go to culinary school. He graduated from Le Cordon Bleu with honors. But at the same time, Sprints was being lured by the siren song of craft beer. He became ingratiated into the scene, joining a homebrew club, the Oregon Brew Crew, and meeting a number of craft beer pioneers. It was a combination of the long, inconsistent hours of the restaurant industry, which kept him from his family, and his interest in the burgeoning and vibrant beer scene, that caused him to replot his career course. In 1993, he made the quality of life decision to open the Hair of the Dog Brewing Company. However, unlike most other breweries at the time, Sprints wanted to provide beer lovers with brews that were new or unique, with a focus on the stylistically unusual. Beers he enjoyed. Driven by creativity, Sprints became one of the first brewers in America to specialize in bottle conditioned and barrel aged beers. The brewery is currently home to 180 oak barrels used to age beer anywhere from six months to eight years. Many of his beers are named in honor of friends and collaborators

> The quality of life decision Sprints made back in 1993 continues to pay dividends. He is now in the process of passing the brewery on to the next generation. He has three sons, and the middle child, Isaac, has been brewing for the past few years.

The tasting room.

who have provided inspiration, including one of the brewery's most popular beers, Fred—named in honor of legendary beer writer and historian, Fred Eckhardt.

In an industry that often chases trends, Hair of the Dog has remained not only relevant, but also among the most respected in the community, primarily because of Sprint's ability to keep producing the beers they started with while staying on the cutting edge of the world beer scene. The brewpub also benefits from Sprint's culinary background. The food menu incorporates local produce and protein with the pub's our own house-made pickles, baked goods, and cured meats. Reflecting Sprint's dedication to supporting the local community, 99 percent of all the ingredients used for food and beverage comes from within a 350-mile radius of the brewery. Hair of the Dog also offers the largest selection of vintage bottles available in the country and a curated draft list with beer fermented or aged in various woods, concrete, and steel. Sprints also enjoys collaboration, noting that beer brings people together. "We are proud of the work we do with brewers from other countries, helping to make the world a smaller place."

61 Southeast Yamhill St.
503-232-6585
hairofthedog.com

A cornerstone for elevated, creative cuisine.

In 2011, Chef/Owner Sarah Pliner opened Aviary along with two other chef/owners on one of Portland's favorite culinary thoroughfares, Alberta Street. Her partners have since moved on. But since then, her wildly creative cuisine has consistently earned Aviary a spot at or near the top of every "Best of" restaurant list in the city. Pliner uses classic French technique in her approach to exotic Asian flavors and the freshest seasonal ingredients she can find. Her success is no accident. She spent decades working in New York and Portland at a number of notable restaurants, including Alain Ducasse at the Essex House, Aquavit, Aldea, Socialista, and the Heathman Restaurant and Bar. It's at Aviary that she's really spread her wings, however, earning a nomination for *Food & Wine*'s People's Best New Chef in 2013, 2014, and 2015, and being named a semifinalist for the James Beard Award for Best Chef Northwest in 2015, 2016, and 2017.

1733 Northeast Alberta St.
503-287-2400
aviarypdx.com

Above left: Chef Sarah Pliner. Photo courtesy of John Valls.

Top right: Artichoke and Quince Tart. Photo courtesy of Carly Diaz.

Above right: Chicken Skin Salad. Photo courtesy of Carly Diaz.

KIM JONG GRILLIN' AND THE KIM JONG SMOKEHOUSE

The Phoenix of food carts, a Korean cult favorite, and then some.

As you could probably ascertain from the cart's name, Chef Han Ly Hwang doesn't take himself too seriously. His food, however, is another story. And what a story it is. By his own admission, Hwang was a bit of a hooligan growing up in Northern Virginia. In fact, he started working in restaurants at the age of fifteen to fulfil probation requirements. He enjoyed cooking, but he wasn't quite ready to dedicate his life to the culinary arts just yet. As an adult, he moved to Portland to snowboard, and he worked in kitchens to support his habit. With his skills sharpening, he became a culinary mercenary around town. When he decided to open his own food cart, it was alcohol-fueled inspiration that led to the play on words, Kim Jong Grillin'. The stellar Korean BBQ being produced by Chef Hwang quickly earned a number of stalwart fans. Then the cart caught fire. Literally.Kim

Though it is still a bit of a mystery exactly how it started, the fire that broke out one night left the cart unrecoverable. Dejected, Hwang began a bit of a downward spiral. As a last-ditch effort to earn some recognition and much-needed cash, he agreed to go on a food cart–themed episode of the popular television show *Chopped*. He performed

> The opening of the Kim Jong Smokehouse came as a bit of a surprise to Hwang. The concept was in place when he went to Mexico on vacation. His partners were pretty motivated, however. When he got back to the US, he discovered that the new restaurant had already been announced.

Left: 2016 Sandwich invitational winning sandwich by Kim Jong Grillin'.
Right: Galbi Bibim Box from Kim Jong Grillin'.

well, making it to the final round before getting dismissed. Though he didn't win, legendarily finicky judge Scott Conant had some very complimentary things to say about Chef Hwang's culinary skill. And off camera, he had even more encouraging things to say, almost insisting that he get back in the game. A few weeks later, the Kim Jong Grillin' cart was reborn, and the airing of the *Chopped* episode kicked the cart's business into high gear. In a town that loves ethnic cuisine as much as it loves happy hour, one dish in particular established itself as the city's favorite hangover cure—the Bibim Box. Hwang's inventive take on the classic bibimbap, the KJG version comes with your choice of BBQ protein on top of jhapchae (a type of Korean potato noodles) and rice and topped with a fried egg. From the cart's success, the brick and mortar Kim Jong Smokehouse was born. A collaboration with Earl Ninsom of Langbaan and the Smokehouse Tavern's BJ Smith, the Kim Jong Smokehouse boasts two locations and a menu of Korean-style street food made with Southern BBQ smoking techniques. Sometimes probation works.

Kim Jong Grillin'
4606 Southeast Division St., 503-929-0522
facebook.comkjgpdx

Kim Jong Smokehouse
413 Northwest 21st Ave., 971-373-8990

126 Southwest 2nd Ave., 503-477-9364
kimjongsmokehouse.com

VITALY PALEY (page 172)

THE SUDRA (page 22)

COUNTRY CAT DINNER HOUSE & BAR (page 24)

FARM SPIRIT (page 48).

CHAMELEON RESTAURANT & BAR (page 54)

PAADEE/LANGBAAN (page 68)

HUBER'S (page 50)

HALE PELE (page 56)

HOLDFAST (page 106)

ATAULA (page 112)

KEN FORKISH (page 122)

KIM JONG GRILLIN' (page 204)

BEAST (page 132)

OX (page 144)

MAE/YONDER (page 162)

QUAINTRELLE (page 166)

HIGGINS (page 124)

AVA GENE'S (page 58)

RINGSIDE STEAKHOUSE AND FISH HOUSE

Portland standouts for almost seventy-five years.

In 1944, the Peterson family, third-generation owners of RingSide Hospitality Group, opened the RingSide Steakhouse in a brick building in Nob Hill. It has retained its status as one of the city's favorite steakhouses and most venerable restaurants ever since. It is home to one of Portland's only onsite dry aging rooms, and the wine selection is top-tier, earning *Wine Spectator*'s Best of Award of Excellence since 2001. Then in 2011, the Peterson family opened RingSide Fish House, the perfect Yin to the steakhouse's Yang. In addition to a menu that features a number of seasonal, local delicacies including oysters, King Salmon, and Dungeness crab, RingSide Fish House proudly sports one of the best early and late-night happy hour menus in Portland. And in a city where the two main religions are brunch and happy hour, that's saying something.

RingSide Steakhouse
2165 West Burnside St.
503-223-1513
ringsidesteakhouse.com

RingSide Fish House
838 Southwest Park Ave.
503-227-3900
ringsidefishhouse.com

Most guests at the steakhouse begin their dining experience with RingSide's legendary world-famous onion rings—James Beard once claimed them to be "the best I've ever had."

Top left: The dining room at RingSide Steakhouse.

Top right: Dry aged beef.

Above left: New York Strip.

Above right: The world-famous and James Beard–approved onion rings.

Progressive, elevated New American cuisine.

The chef/owner of Nomad.PDX, Ryan Fox, is nothing if not driven. Having started with $100 and a dream, he fought for every dollar and modicum of support to shift people's perception of what fine dining is. Through their work, he and his team are forging a new path for food and a new way of connecting through food. Three Navy Seal quotes keep him moving forward: "The only easy day was yesterday. Get comfortable being uncomfortable. Have a shared sense of purpose." To reiterate, Chef Fox is nothing if not driven.

He began working as a dishwasher at the age of thirteen at a local restaurant in Chagrin Falls, Ohio. From there, he worked in various Cleveland-area restaurants before attending the Culinary Institute of America in Hyde Park, New York. After graduation, he took a job at one of Michael Mina's Las Vegas restaurants and then the three Michelin-starred restaurant Joël Robuchon at MGM in Las Vegas. After being there for several years and getting some experience, he decided to move to Portland because of the unique geography and plethora of food available in the Pacific Northwest. He developed a deep understanding of Portland and the region's ingredients while working at one of Portland's most renowned modernist Meccas, Castagna. Along with Chef Ali Matteis, he began a pop-up restaurant and underground supper club in 2014. Finally, in

> "The Pacific Northwest has been my current inspiration for the past several years. There is so much potential in the bounty of the area that it seems to currently be in an infant stage. I want to be a part of refining it and truly making Portland and the area stand out on a world stage."
>
> –Chef/Owner Ryan Fox

Left: Chef Ryan Fox. Photo courtesy of Jordan Fox.

Right: The dining room at Nomad.PDX. Photo courtesy of Jordan Fox.

early 2017, the two opened the brick and mortar Nomad.PDX in Northeast, serving a mind-expanding fifteen-to-twenty course tasting menu, as well as a la carte food service.

The restaurant's layout is also unique, with three distinct areas, each possessing its own vibe and atmosphere. The Chef's Counter is actually in the open kitchen. Guests can sit and watch their food being prepared while chatting with the chefs and learning the stories behind the dishes. The Dining Room is a darker, more intimate setting. And the Ash Bar is a cozy, tucked-away bar in its own room. Three spaces, acting as one laboratory where chefs Fox and Matteis continually strive to make their dishes better. According to Fox, that's what makes them tick. The two have a photo catalog of their food, allowing them to observe the evolution of a dish idea from four years ago up to its present incarnation. Which in turn helps them to redesign dishes by adding ingredients and creating new ones.

575 Northeast 24th Ave.
503-206-4085
nomadpdx.com

HOLDFAST

One of Portland's premier tasting menu restaurants in a new and bigger space.

Joel Stocks, a Portland native, got an early start cooking: One of his best friend's fathers owned a restaurant, and at fifteen, Joel was splitting a full-time cooking job with his friend. Stocks eventually went on to pursue culinary school at the Culinary Institute of America in New York. After school, he worked at Noble Rot and 50 Plates before joining the staff at Park Kitchen.

Will Preisch grew up in the restaurant business. His father ran twenty-four-hour diners in Cleveland, Ohio, from before he was born until after he graduated high school. He started working in the diner in elementary school bussing tables, prepping in middle school, and eventually working on the line. Preisch would also pursue an education in the culinary arts before becoming, in his own words, a proud culinary-school dropout. Preisch moved to Portland in 2005, working at Le Pigeon before moving on to Park Kitchen, where he met Stocks.

The two became fast friends over a shared appreciation of bourbon and a similar culinary vision. In keeping with their passions, the two helped open the Bent Brick. Their modernist take on tavern fare never quite got its legs underneath it, but it allowed Stocks and Preisch to explore, experiment, and innovate. The two left the Bent Brick and Portland for a time, working in kitchens further afield. When they rallied back in Portland, they started exploring modernist menu notions via a pop-up restaurant. With proof of concept firmly in place, they opened Holdfast in 2015. The small, tasting-menu-only restaurant affords diners a front-row seat to the cooking and plating. The chefs interaction with guests throughout the meal is a means of breaking down the barriers between the front of house and

Above left: Holdfast offers white-table dishes in a Portland-casual atmosphere.

Top right: Cuisine inspired by Spanish, Japanese, Thai, American, and beyond.

Above right: A sample tasting menu offering at Holdfast.

the back of house. It's a no-frills, stripped-down dining experience akin to a white tablecloth setting, but in a very casual, very Portland environment—clean, simple, refined, primitive. The menu changes frequently, inspired by local, seasonal produce and drawing on inspiration from a wide array of cuisines, including Spanish, Japanese, Thai, and American.

In 2018, Stocks and Preisch moved Holdfast into a larger space in Southeast, which allowed them to integrate their casual cocktail bar concept, Deadshot, into the fold. The brainchild of friend and former co-worker Adam Robinson, the cuisine is a take on bar food classics, done in a Holdfast style. The new Holdfast is essentially two eateries in one, anchored by an ethos that is helping to pen the next chapter of the Portland food story.

2133 Southeast 11th Ave.
503-504-9448
holdfastdining.com

The pairing of a renowned celebrity chef and one of Portland's own rising culinary stars.

If you've watched any food-based competitive television over the last decade, you've seen Chris Cosentino. Raised in an Italian-American community in Rhode Island, he graduated from Johnson & Wales University and embarked on his culinary career with vigor. He worked at San Francisco's Rubicon, the Coach House on Martha's Vineyard, and the legendary Chez Panisse in Berkley, among others. He moved back to San Francisco to take over executive chef duties at Incanto, simultaneously bringing the restaurant back to prominence while developing what became his culinary signature of whole-animal cooking. Cosentino earned a reputation for transforming offal and other underappreciated morsels into sought-after menu items. In 2007, he appeared as a contestant on the Food Network's *The Next Iron Chef*. In the following years he became a semi-regular on the network, contributing to *The Best Thing I Ever Ate* and co-hosting the show *Chefs vs City*. In 2012 he had his finest television moment, winning Bravo's *Top Chef Masters* by beating out a number of culinary titans and raising $141,000 for charity in the process. Two years later he opened his flagship restaurant, Cockscomb, in San Francisco after Incanto closed.

A different Chef Chris, last name Diminno, is another star on the rise. The native New Yorker attended the Culinary Institute of America, worked around his home city for a while, and then decided it was time for a change of scenery. In 2009 he visited Portland, and despite the rainy weather, he fell in love with the town. Thirty days later he moved. He sent letters out to just about every restaurant in the city looking for work and received exactly two offers—egg cook for Mother's Bistro and sous chef at Clyde Common. The sous position

Top left: Chef Chris Cosentino. Photo courtesy of Aubrie LeGault.

Top right: The Savory Waffle, with butternut squash, smoked fish, creme fraiche, and salmon roe. Photo courtesy of Aubrie LeGault.

Above left: Chef Chris Diminno. Photo courtesy of Aubrie LeGault.

Above right: Oysters. Photo courtesy of Aubrie LeGault.

better matched to what he was looking for. Just eight months later, Diminno took over as executive chef at Clyde Common. During his six-year tenure, Diminno elevated the restaurant into the upper echelon of Portland's ever-improving restaurant scene.

In 2016, Cosentino approached Diminno at Portland's premier food festival, Feast, about teaming up. Diminno was game, and in March of 2017, Jackrabbit opened in the Duniway Hotel. The restaurant's design and layout is visually striking and already award winning. The menu is a continuation of Cosentino's whole-animal approach, accentuated by Diminno's knowledge of Oregon bounty and seasonality. A raw bar, exceptional cocktail menu, and array of house-cured meats are the remaining pieces that make Jackrabbit whole. The restaurant itself might be in its infancy, but the team nurturing it know a thing or two about raising restaurants the right way, as well as the culinary bar.

830 Southwest 6th Ave., 503-412-1800, gojackrabbitgo.com

Chef Gabriel Rucker's flagship restaurant might be Portland's quintessential dining experience.

The list of superlatives that have been used to describe Gabriel Rucker's talent and the restaurant resulting from it is long indeed. Utilizing his talent, timing, and instincts, Rucker opened up Le Pigeon at the age of twenty-five. And in the decade plus since that coming out party, Le Pigeon has, for many, come to exemplify the best of Portland cuisine. It is casually meticulous, all at once hip, refined, and rough around the edges. The French-inspired menu routinely delivers a rare blend of wild creativity and perfect execution.

Rucker grew up in the Napa Valley area—not a bad place to calibrate your palate. He got into cooking because career-wise, nothing else was doing it for him. When he was eighteen, Rucker attended Santa Rosa Jr. College's culinary program for one day before dropping out. He worked around the Napa Valley restaurant scene for a while, drawing inspiration and developing his own culinary style. In 2003, Rucker moved to Oregon, largely because San Francisco was too expensive. He'd heard good things about Portland and decided to give it a go. His timing was excellent: The early 2000s were an exciting and formative time in the annals of Portland cuisine. He landed a job at Paley's Place, where he gained

Chef Rucker has a deep love and appreciation for the California burger chain In-N-Out. Known for its loyal legions, the fast food restaurant remains one of his first stops from the airport when he visits home. Says Rucker, "If I had the opportunity to open up an In-N-Out in Portland, I would definitely cash in everything else and go for that."

Left: Chef Gabriel Rucker. Photo courtesy of Mark-Pratt Russum.
Right: A stunning dessert offering. Photo courtesy of David Reemer.

experience under the tutelage of one of the city's premier chefs, Vitaly Paley. Rucker spent two years with Paley before taking on the role of sous chef at the Gotham Tavern. That's where he met his future sous chef, Erik Van Kley. While there, he also worked with future All Star chefs Tommy Habetz of Bunk Bar and Beast's Naomi Pomeroy. Chef Rucker's journey to stardom culminated with the opening of Le Pigeon in 2006.

That same year, Rucker was named *Portland Monthly*'s Chef of the Year and the *Oregonian*'s Rising Star. He then went for big air, winning the James Beard Award for Rising Star Chef in 2011 and the James Beard Award for Best Chef Northwest in 2013. In 2010 he opened a larger, more casual bistro version of Le Pigeon downtown in the form of Little Bird, and in 2018 he opened Canard, specializing in French bar food, next door to the flagship Le Pigeon on East Burnside.

Le Pigeon
738 East Burnside St., 503-546-8796, lepigeon.com

Little Bird
215 Southwest 6th Ave., 503-688-5952, littlebirdbistro.com

Putting Spanish food on the map in Portland.

José Chesa is a rare bird. He is wholly consumed by both his passion for being a chef, and his intrinsic desire and ability to be a family man. Chesa is quite possibly one of the nicest, most affable, most caring people in Portland. He is also a man dedicated to the art and craft of being an upper echelon chef, and earning everything that comes with it. You can trace both traits back to his father.

Growing up in Spain, the son of a chef, Chesa was literally surrounded by exceptional cuisine. His father worked all day every day at the restaurant he ran for thirty years. Chesa was raised by his mother and grandmother, but his father did his absolute best, despite his work-related absence. Chesa grew up cooking alongside his father at the restaurant and his grandmother at home. It didn't take long for him to decide that his passion and talent for cooking was going to be his career. At the tender age of fifteen, he revealed this plan to his father, who responded by refusing to let Chesa work at his restaurant any longer. If he was going to become a chef, he was going to have to give it his all. So from the ages of fifteen to eighteen, Chesa attended the finest culinary school in Barcelona.

He then went on a worldwide tear, working in Paris, New York, Barcelona, and Puerto Rico for prestigious Michelin-starred

In 2016, Baez and Chesa opened their second restaurant, named Chesa, in honor of his father. Unfortunately, that same winter a series of brutal and unusual snowstorms all but shut the city down. The momentum the restaurant had built up was lost, and the restaurant closed in July 2017. Ataula, however, is just as strong as ever.

Left: Chef José Chesa. Photo courtesy of Brian Balducci.
Right: Dinner at Ataula. Photo courtesy of Carly Diaz.

restaurants including Arpege, Can Fabes, and Fleur-de-Sel, with mentors like Alain Passard, Cyril Renauld, Santi Santamaria, Dominique Bouchet, and Nandy Jubany. He met and fell in love with Cristina Baez, and the two married in her native Puerto Rico, where the couple lived for three years. Then Baez, a graduate of the Culinary Institute of America herself, attended a food stylist workshop in Portland and fell in love with the town. The young couple moved to the Northwest and opened Ataula in 2013, one month before the birth of their first child. In 2016, Chesa cofounded 180, Portland's first xurreria. Then came the accolades. First, in 2014, Chesa was named *Portland Monthly*'s Chef of the Year, and in 2017 he received his second nomination as a semifinalist for Best Chef Northwest by the James Beard Foundation. Somehow, Chesa finds balance. He regularly takes his son to school and brings him to the restaurant for lunch. And in early 2018, Baez and Chesa welcomed their second child into the world. It can't be easy being a top-tier chef or family man, but José Chesa certainly appears to be enjoying both.

1818 Northwest 23rd Pl.
503-894-8904
ataulapdx.com

The man responsible for some of the city's signature restaurants, and then some.

It would not be possible to write the story of food in Portland without including a chapter on Restaurateur/Chef John Gorham. Growing up, Gorham moved around a lot—twenty-one times before graduating high school, to be exact. Throughout his early life, he spent time in Northern California, North Carolina, and Ghana, among other locales. He also really enjoyed cooking. These two factors helped set the stage for one of Portland's true culinary empires.

In 2007 he opened Toro Bravo, exposing Portlanders to the glories of Spanish cuisine and elevated tapas-style small plates. A few years later he opened Tasty n Sons in North Portland. To this day, it is perhaps the reigning heavyweight champ of brunch restaurants in town. In a city where people worship both brunch and happy hour, that's no insignificant task. This "New American Diner" is an ode to Chef Gorham's travels, offering a global collaboration of flavors with a Northwest twist. He later extended the Tasty brand west of the river in the form of the equally successful Tasty n Alder. Next up, the three-time James Beard Award nominee opened the Mediterranean Exploration Company (MEC) in the Pearl District. With Executive Chef Kasey Mills and business partner Ron Avni, Gorham would dive even deeper into Israeli and eastern Mediterranean influences.

To pay homage to their home states of North and South Carolina,

John Gorham's culinary empire expanded in 2018 with the opening of a new Shalom Y'all in Southeast Portland, as well as another Bless Your Heart Burgers.

Left: Korean Fried Chicken at Tasty n Sons. Photo courtesy of Reamer Photography.

Center: Scallops at Toro Bravo. Photo courtesy of Reamer Photography.

Right: Grilled Asparagus with Spanish Ham at Toro Bravo. Photo courtesy of Reamer Photography.

Gorham and Chef Drew Sprouse opened Bless Your Heart Burgers in the new Pine Street Market. It's a place where you can get a perfectly executed American cheeseburger or step up your game with the Carolina burger that adds chili, slaw, and homemade pickles. Taking MEC's inspirations and flavors a step further, Gorham, Mills, and Avni opened Shalom Y'all—a fun and casual establishment offering house-made pita, hummus, falafel, and an exquisite take on the Israeli breakfast standard, shakshuka. And finally, there's Plaza Del Toro, a private event space, test kitchen, and gastronomic society. Like Bruce Wayne has his bat cave, Chef Gorham has Plaza Del Toro.

You could easily attribute John Gorham's success to culinary skill, business acumen, and work ethic—a trifecta of traits in which he most certainly excels. But there's a reason his restaurants are family style dining affairs. Talk to anybody who works or has worked for Gorham and you'll discover that he treats his staff, as well as his guests, like his own flesh and blood. And that might be the real secret to his success.

Plaza Del Toro, 105 Southeast Taylor St.
503-764-9678, plazadeltoropdx.com

shalomyallpdx.com
tastynalder.com
torobravopdx.com

tastynsons.com
byhpdx.com
mediterraneanexplorationcompany.com

One of America's most lauded Russian restaurants.

The daughter of Russian Jewish immigrants, Chef Bonnie Morales grew up on Russian food in the Chicago area. And admittedly, as a child and young adult, she was not the biggest fan of the cuisine. After college she moved to Manhattan, where she worked a soul-crushing job designing cell phones. The allure of the famous Union Square Greenmarket, which was just outside her office, was too much. Once the realization set in that she liked the farmers market more than her job, she quit to attend culinary school. She excelled, and eventually found herself back in Chicago working at top-tier restaurants. While in Chicago, she met a man who not only shared her passion for food and cooking but would later become her husband. Yes, Morales is her married name, just in case you're the sort who needs ethnic assurance regarding cuisine. Morales used to prep him before dinners at her parents' house, harkening back on her own discontent with Russian food. However, each meal earned raves from her husband. This prompted a bit of soul searching followed by a culinary renaissance for Morales.

She began tinkering with Russian food, introducing French technique in an attempt to make it more palatable. She discovered that the depth and balance of flavors were never quite right when she strayed too far from tradition. She also realized not only that

> Morales released a cookbook, *Kachka, a Return to Russian Cooking,* in November 2017. The restaurant moved to a bigger space in spring 2018. Adjacent to the new location is a small Eastern European deli called "Kachka Lavka." The old space will morph into a lounge/happy spot called "Kachinka."

Left: Chef Bonnie Morales. Photo courtesy of Carly Diaz.
Right: Herring under a Fur Coat. Photo courtesy of Carly Diaz.

were there reasons for certain ingredients and cooking methods, but that Russian cuisine was more varied, and further-reaching, than she had ever known or imagined. The seed was planted, and in 2014, Kachka opened in Portland. The restaurant looks and feels warm and inviting—like a modern take on your grandmother's house. There is always a lot of food, laughter, and vodka. All very good things. And there is a lot of thought and purpose behind everything, including the restaurant's name.

As World War II was ramping up, Morales's grandmother narrowly escaped a mass killing that took place at a ghetto in Minsk. Attempting to flee the country, she was passing as a Ukrainian peasant when a Russian official working with the Germans stopped her. Suspecting that she might be Jewish, he challenged her to say the word "duck" in Ukrainian to prove her identity. She didn't speak Ukrainian. But she did know that there was some linguistic overlap between Yiddish and Belarusian. Knowing that it was a gamble but also her only option, she answered "Kachka," which turns out to be the word for duck in Belarusian and Yiddish, as well as Ukrainian. Lucky for all of us.

720 Southeast Grand Ave.
503-235-0059
kachkapdx.com

A neighborhood seafood restaurant and a city favorite.

As a young man growing up in Virginia, David Farrell landed a job bussing tables in an upscale Chinese restaurant. The exotic cuisine was unlike anything he'd eaten as a child. He developed a desire to learn how to create the things he enjoyed, to study and understand dishes and ingredients he was unfamiliar with. At the same time, he was taken by the way a real restaurant functioned—pace, timing, prep, showtime. It all captivated him, and after working a few different roles in the front of the house, he was certain that back on the line was where he wanted to be. So he enrolled in culinary school in Vermont.

After school Farrell really explored the space, working in France, Sante Fe, and San Francisco. He worked for a number of heavy hitters at big restaurants. The locavore movement in San Francisco inspired him, but he also discovered that he preferred smaller-scale restaurants. After helping to open a restaurant in Sante Fe and working in Atlanta to be close to family, he found himself cooking in Mendocino, California. There he met his partner in life as well as business, Jackie Speck, a talented artist and wine buyer. The two

Cabezon's name was inspired by someone Farrell had worked with years ago. When asked what her favorite fish was, she insisted that cabezon was easily the best fish in the ocean. The mildly flavored sculpin fish isn't typically commercially fished, but it is a favorite for northern California anglers. Although Farrell might not entirely agree, the memory of her passionate response to the question stayed with him.

Left: Chef David Ferrell. Photo courtesy of Frances Dyer.

Right: A seasonal seafood entree. Photo courtesy of Frances Dyer.

wanted to strike out on their own but needed the proper setting to do so, which led them to Portland. An almost unparalleled bounty, coupled with the city's affordability, was too good to pass up.

In 2009, they opened Cabezon. Farrell had learned a lot about fish in San Francisco and wanted to open a seafood-centric restaurant. The couple also wanted a cozy neighborhood place that would double as a destination dining option for the rest of the city. The menu at Cabezon is the convergence of methodologies Farrell picked up throughout his career and the inspiration he draws from what is available any given day. Between the local farmers markets and the fishmongers with whom he has developed close relationships, Farrell has a lot to work with. He relies on what he's able to source and not on preconceived notions of what dinner service should look like. The result is a menu that changes daily. Farrell believes that sometimes simpler is better, and he focuses on drawing out flavors through proper execution rather than artistic presentation. That job is handled by Speck, whose art adorns the walls of Cabezon, Portland's favorite neighborhood seafood restaurant.

5200 Northeast Sacramento St.
503-284-6617
cabezonrestaurant.com

STUMPTOWN COFFEE ROASTERS

Kicking off coffee's "third wave."

America has seen three distinct "waves" of coffee. The first wave was essentially a freeze-dried caffeine delivery system. Ready for the pot, and ready for lots of cream and sugar. The second wave, led predominantly by Peet's and Starbucks, introduced fresh-roasted coffee, espresso drinks, and wildly creative misspellings of commonplace names on to-go cups. The third wave was coffee's coming out party as an artisanal foodstuff. Like wine before it, and chocolate after, coffee's third wave was about a high-quality product that was handled as such. It celebrated the terroir of a growing region, down to the individual farm, by thoughtfully roasting and extracting something that was, in an academic sense, still coffee, but which bore little in common with its predecessors in nuance and flavor. Coffee's third wave was led by three roasters—Intelligentsia Coffee & Tea in Chicago, Counter Culture Coffee in North Carolina, and, way out west, Stumptown Coffee Roasters in Portland.

Duane Sorenson grew up in Seattle, but he loved Portland. He had always been a coffee fan, and as cafes began popping up around Seattle, he quit college to take an apprenticeship roasting coffee. The longer he roasted, the deeper he got, eventually paying attention to single-origin beans from farms he thought were producing a superior product with intriguing flavor notes. He discovered profiles that he could accentuate by not roasting the beans for as long as tradition mandated. Suspecting he was onto something, Sorenson packed his bags and moved to Portland to start his own roasting company.

In 1999, Southeast Division was not the destination drive it is now, but it was the perfect spot for Sorenson to open Stumptown

Left: Inside one of Portland's many locations.

Right: Hair Bender, the one that started it all.

Coffee Roasters in an abandoned space that once housed a beauty salon called the Hair Bender. The name inspired what would become Sorenson's signature blend, and it remains the company's most popular to this day. He tended bar at the iconic Horse Brass Pub in the evening to pay for his daytime coffee business. That didn't last very long. As Sorenson continued to seek out exotic beans and cultivate relationships with the farms producing them, Portlanders took notice of just how superior the end product was. Stumptown exploded throughout the 2000s, eventually opening locations in Seattle, New York, Los Angeles, New Orleans, and Chicago. In late 2015, Peet's Coffee purchased Stumptown, which was a bit of a stomach punch for some Portlanders as their beloved hometown roaster seemed to have gone "bigtime." But the fact remains that Sorenson and Stumptown changed the game, paving the way for a legion of world-class roasters. And regardless of ownership, they still make an exquisite cup of coffee.

4525 Southeast Division St. (Original location)
503-230-7702
stumptowncoffee.com

Ex-techie becomes a Portland baking legend.

No one gets into the culinary arts as a means of acquiring wealth. Almost every discipline in the field requires hard work, long hours, dedication, and training, just to break even at the end of the month. In most cases, anything beyond that is gravy. You could make a strong argument that no other career path in the field requires more love of the game than baking. In addition to the aforementioned hardships, artisan bakers have the additional burdens of high labor and ingredient costs to accompany razor-thin profit margins. There's an old French saying that sums it up perfectly—"You have to sell a lot of bread to make a little money." None of that stopped Ken Forkish from becoming Portland's most renowned baker.

Forkish, burnt out on the tech industry, left it all behind to do something he cared about, to hone a craft. Inspiration, at least, was easy. Having spent considerable time in France and other parts of Europe, Forkish fell deeply in love with the broad spectrum of divine breads and pastries found on almost every corner—baked goods he could not find back in the states. After years of study, practice, and training, including an education at the San Francisco Baking Institute, Forkish chose Portland as the place to practice his new trade. In 2001, he opened Ken's Artisan Bakery. Taking no shortcuts, using only the finest ingredients, and making the best of his knowledge and skill, Forkish and his bakery slowly but surely ascended to the top of the Portland baking heap. Wanting to expand his craft and creativity, he opened Ken's Artisan Pizza in 2016, which earned similar acclaim. Forkish penned his first award-winning book, *Flour Water Salt*, in 2012 and opened the Trifecta Tavern & Bakery in 2013. The Trifecta is a triple threat of elevated food, drink, and baked goods, as well as a lab for Forkish to test new ideas and recipes

Tossing dough at Ken's Artisan Pizza. Photo courtesy of Alan Weiner.

before releasing them to the public. Finally, in 2016, he published another well-received book, *The Elements of Pizza*.

Still, the James Beard Award winner and multi-nominee is not content with a good bake. Forkish strives to refine and improve everything, all the time. Though his croissant has been touted by many as the best they've ever had, he just changed the recipe, and has plans to refine the egg-wash application. The things people do for the love of the game.

Ken's Artisan Bakery
338 Northwest 21st Ave.
503-248-2202, kensartisan.com

Ken's Artisan Pizza
304 Southeast 28th Ave.
503-517-9951, kensartisan.compizza

Trifecta Tavern
726 Southeast 6th Ave.
503-841-6675, trifectapdx.com

The chef who started it all.

Portland's first James Beard Award–winning chef, Greg Higgins, launched the whole animal, slow food, farm-to-table approach that became the blueprint for success in the city. If the question is, "Where did it all begin?" the answer is, "Higgins." But elite-level award winners and pioneers aren't born so much as forged. Greg Higgins was raised in a small town forty-five minutes outside of Buffalo, New York. The way he sees ingredients and relates to them started there. He grew up with a garden, he foraged wild edibles, and he often fished for dinner. Later he worked at a farm and then for a local cheesemaker. He also started making his own sausage. And while this might all sound part and parcel to the way things are done in every other Portland restaurant, or the way every other country abroad does things, remember, this was the United States in the '70s, a time when canned, boxed, and beige ruled the landscape and microwaves started replacing ovens.

Higgins cooked his way through art school for a time before moving to Europe to simultaneously broaden his artistic and culinary horizons. When he came back to the United States, he landed in the northwest corner of the continent, where the region's bounty widened his eyes. He worked for a time in Seattle before eventually

Higgins is a proponent of building community through food, occasionally staging charity pizza events at his own home and growing vegetable starts for his customers. Ever the avid gardener, between the produce that is coming into his restaurant and what he grows himself, he's put together a considerable seed bank.

Left: Chef Greg Higgins.
Right: The restaurant exterior.

settling in Portland, where he worked his way up to executive chef at the Heathman. During this time, Higgins focused on developing strong relationships with growers and artisans in a period when those avenues weren't nearly as multitudinous as they are today, or even ten years ago.

In 1994, he opened Higgins Restaurant and Bar. With a focus on local, seasonal, and sustainable cuisine, Higgins officially ushered in a new era. At the same time, and in keeping with his ethos, he became a founding member of the Chef's Collaborative, an organization formed to "promote sustainable cuisine by celebrating the joys of local, seasonal, and artisanal cooking." And in 2002 he won the James Beard Award for Best Chef Northwest. Nothing is constant but change at the restaurant. Today, the menu morphs with the calendar—punctuated by anchor seasonal dishes and influenced by ongoing conversations with farmers and consumers.

1239 Southwest Broadway
503-222-9070
higginsportland.com

KENNY & ZUKE'S DELICATESSEN

A classic Jewish deli in downtown Portland.

It might sound hard to believe. Like a great taco from Vermont, or a stellar Cuban sandwich from North Dakota. Initially, the statement "Outstanding Oregon Reuben" will read just as suspect as those first two claims. But don't tell that to Ken Gordon. It's been more than a decade since Kenny & Zuke's Delicatessen came into being. And in that time, it has become a downtown culinary cornerstone, garnering not just throngs of Portland loyalists, but national attention as well, including kudos from the likes of *Gourmet Magazine* and even the *New York Times*. Says Gordon, "Kenny & Zuke's is a pretty classic Jewish delicatessen. It's the kind of food I grew up on in New York City, and after years of cooking French and a kind of rustic, more personal cuisine, it's ironically the type of food I've been most successful with. And it came about almost completely be accident."

Originally a political science major when the Watergate scandal made headlines, Gordon was put off by his chosen career path. He turned to the culinary arts, and after stints in Boston, the Bay Area, Paris, and his home town of New York, Gordon landed in Portland. Which brings us back to the Reuben from Oregon. "It's become somewhat iconic in a city where there really isn't a natural or historical connection with this kind of food," says Gordon. "Which just points to the universality of this kind of food. And how we do it—when we opened everybody, here and nationally as well, said we were doing something new. But that was just the point—what we were doing wasn't new . . . it was the way delis did it fifty to one hundred years ago. But not many were doing it that way anymore. And that was new. And it fed people's memories of what this food could be if it

Above left: Chef Ken Gordon. The "Kenny" of Kenny & Zuke's.

Top right: The pastrami sandwich.

Above right: Bagel with cream cheese.

were done right. And created new memories for those new to the genre."

Gordon has since added Kenny & Zuke's Bagelworks in Northwest Portland, making, you guessed it, arguably the best bagels in Oregon and beyond. There's also an abbreviated version of the deli in Portland International Airport. Gordon even has eyes on potentially expanding up to Seattle. Who knows, maybe someday the statement "Remarkable Washington Corned Beef" won't cause sideways glances.

Kenny & Zuke's Delicatessen
1038 Southwest Stark St.
503-222-3354
kennyandzukes.com

Kenny & Zuke's Bagelworks
2376 Northwest Thurman St.

LAURELHURST MARKET

Not your father's steakhouse.

Portland values authenticity. The city has a finely tuned BS detector that quickly weeds out false fronts or endeavors that aren't doing things the right way, for the right reasons. It's also not a very dressy town. For example, business casual attire typically means a collar is involved and most of your toes are hidden. Hiking pants and boots qualify. In a town that possesses those two traits, it's not surprising that the Laurelhurst Market has become the gold standard for steakhouses. The neighborhood haunt combines a butcher shop and a wide-open restaurant with an atmosphere that is warm, inviting, casual, and wafting with the divine aromas of smoke and grill. The menu is loaded with some of the best house-made, house-stuffed, and house-smoked products in the city. Of course, it didn't happen by accident. The team behind the meat is formidable.

The "Your Neighborhood Restaurant Group" is headed by Chef/ Owners David Kreifels, Jason Owens, and Benjamin Dyer. The triumvirate is also responsible for some other beloved Portland dining establishments through the years, including the Simpatica Dining Hall, Reverend's BBQ, and Ate-Oh-Ate. In 2014, they named Benjamin Bettinger as executive chef at the Laurelhurst Market, and in 2016 he became part owner and brought in Jon

> In 2017, Bettinger, along with the "Your Neighborhood Restaurant Group," opened Big's Chicken, based around the popular chicken dish he would occasionally serve for staff. Just weeks after getting off the ground, the establishment was lost in a business-ending fire. Bettinger wasn't about to let it go, however. The restaurant was reborn in Beaverton in 2018.

Left: Chef/Owner Benjamin Bettinger.

Right: A sampling of dinner items.

Anderson of Le Pigeon fame to shore up the line as sous chef. They've been firing on all cylinders since, being named the city's Best Steakhouse by the *Oregonian* in 2017. If you run down Bettinger's pedigree, it was just a matter of time.

At the age of nineteen, the Vermont native was working as a dishwasher in a restaurant when the manager threw him on the line. The people, the frenetic pace, and the feeling of nailing a dinner service was all an ADD kid's dream, and he took to it like a fish to water. The young man who finished near the bottom of his class in high school moved to Portland and graduated second in his class from the Western Culinary Institute. He then landed a coveted internship with Portland culinary legend Vitaly Paley. By his own admission, Bettinger was never the most talented chef on the line, but nobody was going to outwork him. After testing his mettle during his externship, Paley hired Bettinger, who steadily worked his way up to chef de cuisine. By that time, his skill had caught up to his work ethic. He left Paley's Place for the position of executive chef at the critically acclaimed Beaker & Flask before returning to help Paley open the Imperial. He ran the show at the Imperial for two years before accepting his position at the Laurelhurst Market. And steak dinners in Portland haven't been the same since.

3155 East Burnside St.
503-206-3097, laurelhurstmarket.com

Authentic Indian spice blends in East Portland.

Despite any impressions you might gather from the restaurant's name or playful website, Portland's Bollywood Theater offers nothing in the way of otherworldly exuberant dance numbers. What it does offer is an equally authentic Indian experience, pressed gently through a Portland filter. When Chef/Owner Troy MacLarty traveled to India for the first time, he was taken by how prevalent street food is within the nation's culinary culture. The discovery became inspiration, and after honing his skills at the legendary Chez Panisse, his inspiration translated into the Bollywood Theater restaurant on Northeast Alberta. Beyond the food, the décor is more Mumbai than Oregon. The restaurant has been successful thanks to a multi-pronged attack of local produce sourcing, local wine and beer selections, fresh preparations, authentic dishes, and seasonal menu specials. So successful that Bollywood opened a second location on Southeast Division Street in 2014.

2039 Northeast Alberta St.
971-200-4711

3010 Southeast Division Street
503-477-6699
bollywoodtheaterpdx.com

The Southeast Division location is also home to Bollywood Theater's Indian market. Products are personally curated by Chef MacLarty, and recipes for some of his most popular dishes are posted throughout for people to replicate at home. Goods include an extensive selection of Indian spices and pulses, Basmati rice, ghee, Bollywood Theater's own line of masalas, and paneer cheese, freshly made on site six times a week.

Top: Saag Paneer. Photo courtesy of Carly Diaz.

Above left: The interior at the Alberta Street Bollywood.

Above right: Chef Troy MacLarty. Photo courtesy of John Clark.

Portland cuisine, defined.

Born and raised in Corvallis, Oregon, Naomi Pomeroy has the Willamette Valley in her blood. Her early culinary influence was her mother, who spent her early years in Rouen, France, and grandmother Vivian, who hailed from New Orleans. In 1999 and at the age of twenty-four, Pomery and Michael Hebb started Ripe Catering and soon thereafter launched an underground supper club in their Northeast Portland bungalow called "Family Supper." The not-so-legal operation was well-received and prompted a rapid succession of successful and Multnomah County–approved endeavors, starting with the Gotham Coffee Shop in 2002, followed by Clarklewis in 2004, and finally the Gotham Tavern in 2005. By mid-2007, all three establishments had been sold or closed, and along with Mika Paredes, a former pantry cook, Pomeroy started up with small family style suppers again. They added only two servers, and without prep cooks or even a dishwasher, they opened Beast on September 27 of that year.

The twenty-four-seat communal table restaurant serves a six-course, prix-fixe menu as well as two four-course brunch services and dinner on Sunday. The menu changes every other week, based on product availability from the farmers markets and vendors. Beast helped create the blueprint for the set-menu, communal experience that has become one of the city's calling cards. Without a hood or open flame, everything was cooked on two electric induction burners for the first three years of the restaurant's existence. But hurdles and inconveniences proved to have no effect whatsoever on Pomeroy's cuisine and influence on Portland's culinary scene. *Bon Appètit* named her one of the top six of a new generation of female chefs in September 2008, and *Food & Wine Magazine* recognized her as one of the 10 Best New Chefs in America for 2009. She has given

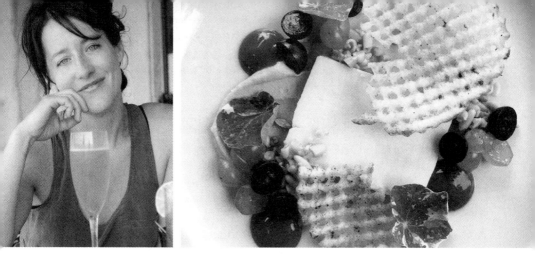

Left: Chef/Owner Naomi Pomeroy. Photo courtesy of Kyle Webster.
Right: Dinner at Beast is a set, six-course dinner based on seasonal availability.

several lectures on creativity, including a TedX talk given in 2013. *Portland Monthly* voted Naomi Chef of the Year in 2008, the same year Beast was honored as Restaurant of the Year by the *Oregonian* and chosen as Best Brunch by the *Willamette Weekly*. In 2010, 2012, and 2013, she was selected as a finalist for the James Beard Awards in the category Best Chef Pacific Northwest before winning the award in 2014.

With her husband, Kyle Webster, Naomi opened Expatriate in 2013. Featuring cocktails overseen by Webster and Southeast Asian drinking snacks created by Pomeroy, it's located right across the street from Beast. In 2016, Naomi's first cookbook, *Taste & Technique: Recipes to Elevate Your Home Cooking*, garnered yet another James Beard Media Award for Styling and Photography.

Beast
5425 Northeast 30th Ave.
503-841-6968
beastpdx.com

Expatriate
5424 Northeast 30th Ave.
503-867-5309
expatriatepdx.com

The Northwest's first signature pork restaurant and the comeback story of 2017.

In a city that exalts all things swine, it makes perfect sense that the first signature pork produced in the Northwest was born in Portland. Across the globe are regional, artisanal products with reputations for excellence: Parmigiano Reggiano from Italy, Kobe beef from Japan, Champagne from France, and the list goes on. Oregon farmer Aaron Silverman wanted to do the same for pork in the Northwest, and he accomplished it with Tails & Trotters. The renowned Jamón Ibérico ham inspired the idea. In Spain, the black-footed, or pata negra, pigs freely roam the region's oak groves while being naturally fattened on acorns. While the Northwest isn't exactly a great place to grow acorns, Oregon is hog heaven for hazelnuts. So, Silverman sources pigs from Pure Country Pork in Ephrata, Washington, and finishes them on hazelnuts from George Packing Company in Newberg, Oregon. The result is a full line of more than a hundred specialty products and cuts with a flavor that is uniquely Pacific Northwest. Tails & Trotters has become the pork of choice for a number of local eateries, including Toro Bravo, Ava Gene's, and Castagna, as well as restaurants nationwide. In late 2012, what started out as a farmers market favorite became a brick-and-mortar butcher shop in Northeast Portland, complete with a sandwich counter.

In 2014, the restaurant unveiled its Prosciutto Pacifico. The culmination of the intent of the business and a recipe that was ten years in the making, the two-year aged meat of the gods won a Good Food Award in the charcuterie category in 2017. But then, in the middle of the night on February 22 of that same year, an electrical fire erupted inside the Northeast shop. The blaze made its way through the lobby and the butcher shop/sandwich counter before it melted a water line, extinguishing the fire. But the heat and smoke rendered

Above left: The exterior of the original location. Photo courtesy of Adam Sawyer.

Top right: The interior of the original location. Photo courtesy of Adam Sawyer.

Above right: Banh Mi sandwich. Photo courtesy of Adam Sawyer.

almost everything that wasn't touched by fire unusable or otherwise destroyed, including three years' worth of aged-pork inventory. A food cart that continued serving its sandwiches kept the business alive and in the public eye. And thanks to insurance, fundraisers launched by local restaurants, and a crowd-sourcing campaign, the lost inventory was slowly rebuilt. Tails & Trotters reopened with a redesigned shop in March 2018, adding more seating and display space.

525 Northeast 28th Ave.
503-477-8682
tailsandtrotters.com

One of Portland's favorite noodle houses.

Go out to eat in just about any city in America these days and you will no doubt encounter certain buzzwords, like "seasonal" and "local." Which is great. It's the way Americans used to eat. And the way that humans, until very recently, always ate—you ate what was around you right now. In some regions of the world, that way of sourcing, preparing, and consuming food never changed. Thailand, for example.

Tonia Ponlakhkan and Tue Sawasdibood came to the United States from Bangkok. The friends shared a passion for food, and in particular, Thailand's seasonal bounty. After Sawasdibood graduated from culinary school, the two moved to Los Angeles. In southern California they discovered a thriving Thai food scene, but not necessarily the right scene for them. The successful restaurants had opulent dining rooms and expensive menu items that matched the cost of leasing space in a California strip mall. After working in several restaurants around town, they moved up to Portland. In the Northwest they discovered not only cheaper rent, but also a food scene lacking the Thai food they knew and loved from Bangkok. So in 2012, they added another business partner, Max Tan, and opened the Nudi Noodle Palace.

The menu is anchored by one constant no matter the season, Nudi's crowd-pleasing Lak Sa—a soup bowl with noodles, pork, prawns, an Onsen poached egg, cilantro, sprouts, fried shallots, onions, and peanut sauce. To the best of anybody's knowledge, it was the first restaurant in Portland to produce the southeast Asian standard.

The Murtabark, or Indian Crepe, at Nudi.

It didn't take long for Nudi to get noticed. Woodstock is a quintessential Portland neighborhood with local shops and restaurants, bungalows, and a laid-back, community-oriented vibe. When Nudi opened with its birdhouse-themed, faux-nature vibe enveloping both the interior and exterior, it was hard not to notice. But the hyper-seasonal menu that made great use of Northwest bounty to infuse local flavor into Thai classics made it a hit. And the same approach taken with the food carries over into the equally seasonal and inventive cocktail offerings, which also utilize house-infused liquors and herbs that act as flavor enhancers with medicinal properties. The menu also extends beyond the traditional Thai, however, with ever-changing offerings that incorporate a broad span of global influences, including Japanese, Malaysian, Korean, and even Italian. Thanks to the well-executed melding of exotic flavor profiles with local ingredients, the Nudi Noodle Palace has become a Woodstock staple and a Portland favorite.

4310 Southeast Woodstock Ave.
503-477-7425
nudipdx.com

Portland's bellwether high-end dining experience.

Culinarily, if there's a hole in Portland's game it's high end. A handful of restaurants sniff at it or produce an elevated tasting menu but still veer towards a slightly more casual dining atmosphere. For years, the one true high-end restaurant in Portland has been, and still is, Castagna. The team propelling the establishment into that rarified air is Owner Monique Siu, Pastry Chef Geovanna Salas, Wine Director Brent Vaughn, and Executive Chef Justin Woodward.

Woodward grew up in San Diego with a father and grandmother who were great in the kitchen. His culinary career started with stints at a bagel place, a deli, and a steakhouse, where he flailed a bit, but was officially bitten by the cooking bug. He attended culinary school at the Art Institute of San Diego before securing a job at L'Auberge Del Mar, where he worked for two and a half years. When the restaurant shut down for renovation, he moved to New York, staging and then working for molecular gastronomy god Wylie Dufresne at wd-50. Woodward followed that up with a staging turn at Copenhagen's legendary Nomo before returning home to San Diego.

Chef Matthew Lightner was working at the L'Auberge Del Mar by then and began conspiring with Woodward to join forces on a more modern project. The two found Castagna in Portland and made the move to the Northwest. Woodward helped Lightner get the kitchen up and running, but then Lightner left the West Coast to work at New York's Atera. So in 2011, Woodward took over the reins at Castagna and has been pushing the modernist envelope ever since. In that time, the James Beard Foundation has taken notice, nominating Woodward once for Rising Star and four times for Best Chef Northwest. And in 2018, he started overseeing the menu at the more accessible Cafe Castagna next door.

Top: Chef Woodward plating a course. Photo courtesy of Alan Weiner.

Above left: Another inventive spring offering. Photo courtesy of Alan Weiner.

Above center: Chef Justin Woodward. Photo courtesy of Alan Weiner.

Above right: Morel mushroom is the star of this spring course. Photo courtesy of Alan Weiner.

1752 Southeast Hawthorne Blvd.
503-231-7373
castagnarestaurant.com

One of Portland's most beloved and storied pizzerias is in a building with more than a few stories itself.

As you might expect, Portland was a much different town in the late 1800s. It simultaneously supported a port economy and a logging industry. As a result, a lot of young, transient men made their way to and from the city. It was a rough, male-dominated town with all the era-appropriate trappings to go along with it: prostitution, drinking, gambling, opium consumption, even crimping, or Shanghaiing, as it would come to be known, were all commonplace. These vices were especially common in the part of town known as Whitechapel or the Old North End, now Old Town/Chinatown. In the heart of it all was the Merchant Hotel. Opened in 1880, the building has largely withstood the test of time, and it has birthed more than a few legends. Not the least of which is the story of Nina. A prostitute servicing the clientele of the hotel, she was found dead at the bottom of the building's elevator shaft. It is believed that she was trying to barter her way out of a life of prostitution at the time, and some believe she haunts the building to this day.

In sunnier times, the Accuardi family converted the lobby of the old hotel into Old Town Pizza (OTP) in 1974. With much of the original layout still in place, the pizzeria is heavy with ambiance. The old hotel reception desk is now the window where patrons order food and drink. Through much of the 1970s, members of Portland's counterculture broke bread here. Willem Dafoe was a regular, as was Trail Blazers center Bill Walton, who routinely ordered a large vegetarian and a pitcher of Henry's. Adam Milne celebrated his ninth birthday at Old Town Pizza, and a lifelong

Great pizza, great beer, great setting.

love affair with the historic haunt followed. He had grown up and into a thriving career with Adidas when he saw that the Accuardi family was putting the business up for sale. It was 2003, and in the year and a half since the attacks of September 11, the restaurant industry as a whole was slumping. Milne, not wanting to see the pizzeria of his youth fade into the ether, acted on instinct and followed his heart. He borrowed against his house, quit his corporate job, and bought Old Town Pizza.

Since then, Milne has shepherded the business into a new era while keeping all of its historic character. The menu of pizza, pastas, and salads remains as strong as ever. And in 2008, he built a second location in Northeast Portland that became the award-winning Old Town Brewing. Milne has also added bicycle delivery to the repertoire, making it the first craft brewery in America to deliver its own beer, as well as pizza, by bicycle. Thank goodness for childhood birthday parties.

226 Northwest Davis St.
503-222-9999
otbrewing.com

One of Portland's Peruvian food pioneers continues to thrive.

In 2003, the Platt-Rodriguez family opened Andina in Portland's Pearl District. The idea was to put forth a menu that balanced Criollo traditions and techniques with modern Peruvian cuisine. Additionally, co-owner Doris Rodriguez and her kitchen staff wanted to showcase the wonderful ingredients that the Northwest had to offer. To that end, they were also one of the first purveyors of ethnic cuisine in the city that embraced local ingredients as a means of complementing native traditional flavors. Andina works closely with farms in Oregon and Peru that grow products specifically for the restaurant. For example, Peace Seedlings organic farm in Corvallis, and Stefan Bedersky, a German-Peruvian who owns an organic farm in the dry, hot southern district of Chincha, Peru, where the restaurant sources its aji chiles. It's proven to be a successful approach, as Andina has remained in the upper echelon of beloved Portland eateries for a decade and a half.

1314 Northwest Glisan St.
503-228-9535
andinarestaurant.com

Portland has a well-earned reputation for catering to dietary restrictions. A happy coincidence for Andina, as Peruvian ingredients and cooking methods naturally lend themselves towards easily accommodating gluten-free, celiac-sensitive, vegetarian, and vegan needs without sacrificing taste.

Top: Arroz con Mariscos.

Above left: Escabeche de Pollo.

Above right: Peppers Ajis. Photo courtesy of David Reamer.

Driven by a husband and wife chef team, the Argentine-inspired Ox is one of Portland's best restaurants.

Greg Denton never wanted to be a firefighter or a policeman. He wanted to be a chef. Born in Schenectady, New York, before moving to Vermont, Denton was the son of a restaurant manager, which gave him access to kitchens. His affinity for food carried into adulthood, leading him to the Culinary Institute of America. After graduating, he worked the circuit—Washington, DC, Ohio, Vermont, and Maine—before landing in Napa Valley, California, at a restaurant called Terra, where he met another young chef named Gabrielle Quiñónez.

Gabrielle Quiñónez grew up in Los Angeles, where she experienced a broad swath of cuisine early on. And despite the fact that her family was full of great home cooks, she didn't fancy the idea of a culinary career right away. She thought that a job in the kitchen might make for a great second career, but as time passed she fell further and further in love with cooking. She got a job at a restaurant with the intention of testing the waters, just to see if it had any appeal. It didn't take long for Quiñónez to decide that the second career was going to become the primary, and she found her way to the California Culinary Academy in San Francisco. Upon graduating, she got a job in Napa Valley, where she met Denton.

The two fell in love while simultaneously moving up the ranks in the kitchen. They married and moved to Maui where they worked for five years. In search of more culinary variety and the possibility of owning their own restaurant, the couple chose Portland as their new home. They worked as co-chefs at Metrovino, and when the opportunity came to do their own thing, they took advantage. Greg

The dining room at Ox.

Denton and Gabrielle Quiñónez Denton opened Ox in 2012. The super duo earned instant accolades for their inspired Argentine cuisine, and in 2016 they opened Superbite downtown as an ode to what they loved about tapas and different culinary influences. Meanwhile, as Ox established itself over the next half decade, the awards and nominations piled up, culminating with the 2017 James Beard Award for Best Chef(s) Northwest. In 2018, the couple repurposed Superbite into a classic, straight-up French Bistro called Bistro Agnes. There's a lot of love going on behind the pass at Ox and Bistro Agnes, and it translates to the plates.

Ox
2225 Northeast Martin Luther King Jr. Blvd.
503-284-3366
oxpdx.com

Bistro Agnes
527 Southwest 12th Ave.
503-222-0979
bistroagnes.com

CHEESE BAR/ CHIZU

Some of the world's finest cheeses elevated into an artform.

After discovering that an art degree wasn't going to pay the bills as well as he'd hoped, Steve Jones turned to cooking to make money. He went to culinary school in Portland and cooked professionally for a short time before helping a friend open a deli. The cheese counter wound up being a game changer for Jones. He became obsessed with the world of cheese. That obsession eventually led to the Cheese Bar and Chizu.

After getting his feet wet in the industry working at Provvista and New Seasons, he opened Steve's Cheese within the Square Deal Wine Company. Once he attained full monger status, Jones struck out on his own. He had always wanted to incorporate beer and cider with cheese, and with the opening of the Cheese Bar, he accomplished just that. The cut-to-order cheese counter features more than two hundred select offerings from near and far, as well as a number of exquisite food and drink pairings. Then in 2015 he opened Chizu, with its remarkably inventive presentation of cheese and accompaniments via a sushi-style ordering card or an omakase, name-your-price format. And it wouldn't be a Steve Jones creation without perfectly paired sake, cider, and beer offerings, of course.

Some of the most well known restaurants and brewpubs in Portland have relied on Jones's cheese prowess for years, including Le Pigeon, Beast, and the Commons Brewery.

Top left: A masterfully assembled board of cheese and accoutrements.

Top right: A smaller, single-cheese offering.

Above left: The interior at Chizu.

Above right: A deluxe spread at Chizu.

Cheese Bar
6031 Southeast Belmont St.
503-222-6014
cheese-bar.com

Chizu
1126 Southwest Alder St.
503-719-6889
chizubar.com

Cuban Creole made from scratch, made with love, and served with pride.

If you explore the city at all, it's hard to imagine that Portland is located anywhere other than the Pacific Northwest. Cloud cover, Douglas fir trees, and moss-accented sidewalks ensure that you know exactly what part of the world you're in. But if you happen to be walking by the Apambichao Building on a warm summer day, it's possible to suspend belief momentarily and imagine that you're on the streets of Havana. For the duration of a meal, anyway.

Pambiche has been serving Cuban comfort food from the brightly colored, turn-of-the-century Victorian landmark since Valentine's Day of 2000. Chef/Owner John Maribona started working for his Cuban godmother Zurina's Latin American food stall, Las Delicias, when he was in high school. After working for her, he started washing dishes in a pie house and eventually began baking the pies. Maribona caught the baking bug and took off. Working at a number of bakeries and dessert houses around town, he became well versed in all aspects of the craft: cookies, cakes, breads, pastries, and everything in between. After baking for six years, he was awarded the pastry chef role at the Greenwood Inn. There, he began to develop his own cooking style. Along with influence from his godmother and inspiration from his grandmother, Abuela Ninf, Maribona infused his own understanding of flavors and cooking technique to sow the

"The biggest culinary inspiration of my life is my Cuban grandmother, Abuela Ninfa. My mother, Ivonne, comes close, but nothing doing, Abuela was head and shoulders above!"
–Chef/Owner John Maribona

Above left: Pambiche and the Apambichao Building.

Top right: Arroz con Pollo.

Above right: Inside Pambiche.

seeds for what would eventually become the menu at Pambiche. In 1995, Maribona moved from pastry to savory and in 1998 from chef to barman. Then in 2000, he opened Pambiche.

Pambiche is what is referred to in Cuba and other parts of the Caribbean and Latin America as a *fonda*—a hole-in-the-wall eatery. However, unlike a typical *fonda*, Pambiche offers an extensive menu like that of a diner. At the same time, Pambiche feels a lot like a typical neighborhood Spanish cafe with its giant espresso machine front and center, bottles of booze lining the back bar, and glowing pastry case in the middle of the dining room. The corner of Northeast Glisan and 28th Avenue might not be Havana, but it sure does look, smell, and feel like it could be. Especially after a few Mojitos and a plate of Camarones al Ajillo.

2811 Northeast Glisan St.
503-233-0511
pambiche.com

Portland's best burger might very well come from a food cart on the fringe of town.

Don Salamone has put in time at multiple Michelin-starred restaurants, but no brioche buns, marrow-infused patties, or house-cured anything can be found at Burger Stevens. Instead, the Southwest Portland food cart serves a classic American cheeseburger. The ingredients are pretty straight forward: toasted Franz buns, Tillamook cheese, Creekstone Farms ground beef. A second Burger Stevens cart just opened in Portland's living room, Pioneer Courthouse Square. If the vibrant powder-blue cart with red lettering doesn't draw customers, the wafting aroma of grilled meat most certainly will.

Hillsdale
6328 Southwest Capitol Way
971-279-7252

Pioneer Courthouse Square
701 Southwest 6th Ave.
503-387-9577
burgerstevens.com

Chef Salamone has an innate ability to find foot traffic. With one cart in the heart of downtown and another backed right up against a high school, he's guaranteed himself a captive audience.

Above: The classic burger with the addition of a roasted jalapeno. Photo courtesy of Adam Sawyer.

Left: Chef/Owner Don Salamone.

STACKED SANDWICH SHOP

One of the Portland's premier chefs making some of the best sandwiches in town.

Chef Gabriel Pascuzzi is a rare commodity in a few ways. To start with, he was born here. He's also not afraid to carve his own path. The Southwest Portland native discovered his love for the kitchen at his uncle's restaurant in Montana. The combination of the pace, the comradery, and the food drew him in, and the time spent working and cooking in a small Montana town helped Pascuzzi discover a real connection to food—that where it comes from and how it's prepared make a difference. After high school he attended the Johnson & Wales College of Culinary Arts in Denver, leaving to work after attaining his two-year degree. He served stints in Austin and Portland before returning to finish school and move on to Italy. He then proved himself under the likes of Tom Colicchio in New York and even staged at the legendary Noma in Copenhagen.

Pascuzzi briefly assumed the role of operating manager at Portland's legendary Whiskey Library, took some time off to explore Asia, and then went to visit a friend in Washington, DC. During his time in the Nation's Capital, he ate at a number of esteemed restaurants and realized that the Portland cuisine scene was as good or better, and the cost of living was infinitely cheaper. So he chose to come back home, joking with his father that it would be fun to open a sandwich shop. The idea was met with familial consternation. However, when the right space and opportunity in Southeast presented itself, Pascuzzi pulled the trigger, and in February 2017, the Stacked Sandwich Shop was born.

A bold move? Certainly. But it was a quality of life move that would allow the chef, along with his staff, more time away from the kitchen. Equally, after years of fine-dining experience, he was

A trio of Stacked sandwiches.

certain that he could take those same sensibilities and produce an evolving lineup of elevated classics, complemented by game-changing, outside-of-the-box creations. Like the Oxtail French Dip. On occasion, he would take a well-known dish and morph it into handheld form. Like the Coq Au Vin sandwich, currently in the blueprint stage. It's about taking the core elements of a dish and translating them. And despite some initial trepidation from those who think the words "chef" and "sandwich" shouldn't coexist in the same brick-and-mortar undertaking, anyone who has enjoyed a meal at Stacked knows those doubts to be unjustified, as does the culinary go-to resource, Eater. They named Pascuzzi Portland Chef of the Year for 2017.

1643 Southeast 3rd Ave.
971 279 2731
stackedsandwichshop.com

Nordic-inspired restaurants, still gaining momentum more than a decade after starting.

Being from the Midwest and of Swedish lineage, Peter Bro grew up knowing the value of good comfort food. While attending the University of Wisconsin-Madison, Bro helped manage a bar, giving him his first taste of the service industry and helping him develop the management skills that would come in handy later in life. In 1996, Bro moved to Portland and picked up where he left off, working his way around town before taking over the bar Aalto Lounge, named for Finnish architect and designer Hugo Alvar Henrik Aalto. Bro also had a background in construction and interior design, so the establishment satiated his interest in both food and architecture. And while the bar's namesake was Finnish, the cuisine was decidedly non-Nordic.

Noting the void, he opened the Broder Cafe in 2007. The breakfast and lunch eatery sported a menu of mostly Swedish and Danish specialties, with some Finnish influence as well. Bro's pan-Nordic cuisine took traditional dishes and infused them with fresh, local

"One thing I have really noticed is this extension of the New Nordic cuisine and culture in general. There is an appeal of the cleanness of the food and simplicity of the dishes' architecture. And, what I like about it is that it hasn't gone away. It's been really nice to experience the staying power or the stickiness of people really appreciating the culture, and that has helped us. It's had a ten-year run, and there's no signs of it dying out."

–Peter Bro, Owner of the Broder restaurants

Brunch spread. Photo courtesy of Jeremy Pawlowski.

ingredients. Because the Nordic and Pacific Northwest climates are somewhat similar, he could source seafood and produce that was akin to the traditional dishes, but with a Northwest bend. He had a hit on his hands. And thanks to the popularity of the cafe, the Broder empire has grown significantly over the last half decade with the addition of three more restaurants: Broder Nord in 2012, Broder Söder in 2015 in the new Nordic Northwest's cultural center Nordia House, and Broder Øst, which opened in 2016 in Hood River.

Broder Cafe, 2508 Southeast Clinton St., 503-736-3333

Broder Nord, 2240 North Interstate Ave., 503-282-5555

Broder Söder, 8800 Southwest Oleson Rd., 503-373-8762

Broder Øst, 102 Oak St. #100, Hood River, 541-436-3444, broderpdx.com

Elegant and elevated New American seafood in a tasting menu format.

A talented, fifth-generation Northwest restaurateur with a drive to excel in all tasks is a good starter kit for success. However, Trent Pierce is as selfless and unassuming as he is gifted, and that might be his secret weapon. He doesn't want a large restaurant, and his staff takes home bigger paychecks than he does. Pierce's end goal isn't a house full of gilded statues. It's to have guests say that they just experienced the best dish of their lives. The food, the guests, the employees, take precedence. Add that on top of lineage, and the success of Chef Pierce and his restaurant, Roe, makes even more sense.

Pierce grew up in and around the restaurant industry. In fact, his grandfather co-owned the *River Queen*—the legendary ferry boat turned restaurant on the Willamette in downtown Portland. As a young man he showed great promise as a runner. He was part of the lauded track program at the University of Oregon, with eyes on the 2008 Olympics in China. When injury prevented that dream from going any further, he focused on a new one, cooking. Pierce observed that Portland's culinary landscape was dominated by meat—pork, beef, charcuterie, offal. It was all about land animals and the return to farm to table, but there was a noticeable void when it came to seafood. Paired with Portland's proximity to the bounty of the Pacific and the rivers that flow into it, seafood became the obvious choice for his culinary voice. So he worked around for a while before opening his first restaurant, Fin, on Southeast Hawthorne. Then Pierce met Kurt Huffman and Ben Blank, heavy hitters in the Portland food scene, and the three of them opened Wafu—a Japanese/ramen restaurant. Wafu wasn't quite as seafood-focused as Pierce wanted, so he opened Roe in the backroom of Wafu.

Top: Chef Trent Pierce and Chef de Cuisine Patrick, plating. Photo courtesy of Alan Weiner Photography.

Above left: Butterfish Sashimi. Photo courtesy of Alan Weiner Photography.

Above right: Scallop and Nairagi. Photo courtesy of Alan Weiner Photography.

Word of mouth spreads quickly in a town like Portland, and it didn't take long for stories of an insanely inventive speakeasy-style seafood restaurant within a restaurant to create a buzz. In short order, Roe gained a reputation for producing beautiful, creative seafood dishes that were unlike anything else in Portland and beyond. James Beard Award nominations followed, and the demand for a tasting menu dinner at Roe continued to grow. So in early 2018, the restaurant moved into a larger but still intimate space in downtown with the idea of making the guest experience even better. It makes sense. It's certainly in keeping with his recipe for success.

515 Southwest Broadway, Suite 100
503-232-1566
roepdx.rest

Farm to table taking a few steps further into food awareness and philanthropy.

Sometimes it takes a while to find your calling. Erika Polmar fell into her current business because of layoffs and an inability to sit still. She graduated with a degree in communications and moved to Portland four days later. Polmar worked briefly selling advertising for the *Willamette Week* but was ultimately let go and moved on to temp work, then event planning. After her first true love and best friend died, she quit her job, bought a jeep, and drove all over the Northwest. When she returned to Portland, she scrambled for work, ultimately ending up in tech. In 2001, shortly after the terrorist attacks of 9/11, she was let go. The weekend after losing her job, she was at a friend's winery helping to sort grapes when she learned that Vitaly Paley and a group of Portland chefs wanted to put on a fundraising dinner for children orphaned by the

"My goal with Plate & Pitchfork is to change people's purchasing practices, to support local sustainable farmers & producers, and to end hunger in Oregon. That last part is the trickiest because the problem requires more than just money to fix. For my part, I started Plate & Pitchfork Fund to End Hunger with the MRG Foundation. We award funds to nonprofits that are finding creative solutions to our food insecurity problem. This past year we supported three organizations, one of which was Farmers Ending Hunger—they can feed a family of four their recommended daily allowance of fruits and vegetables for an entire year with only $150. It's incredible."

—Erika Polmar, Founder/Owner of Plate & Pitchfork

Above left: Carman Ranch beef, hitting the grill.

Top right: A typical dining room at a Plate & Pitchfork dinner.

Above right: Touring the farm before dinner.

collapse of the twin towers. They needed an organizer, and Polmar fit the bill. The event, called Flux, was a hit. She was electrified, and now also had a number of contacts in the food and wine industry.

While planning another event, her former business partner regaled her with stories of beautiful community suppers in Italy. Polmar thought she could do something similar in the Willamette Valley, especially given the similarities in climate. She had also recently discovered that 90 percent of kids graduating from high school couldn't trace their food source past the grocery store. There was a disconnect between eaters and food—something she wanted to remedy. In addition, she wanted to raise money to help ensure that all Oregonians had access to healthy food. Polmar started Plate & Pitchfork, a mission-driven business that fell right into her wheelhouse.

Sixteen years later, Plate & Pitchfork offers ten to twelve farm dinners every summer. Each features two chefs and a winery on a farm. No two dinners are the same. Guests start their evening with a farm tour and sit down for dinner in the middle of a field, where they enjoy a four to five course meal prepared with produce from the fields they just toured. Proceeds from each event go to help end hunger in Oregon. Over the course of the dinner, guests learn about all of the people involved in crafting the meal—the chefs, farmer, baker, winemaker, rancher, fisherman. But that education comes in the form of conversation, not lecture. Polmar's goal is that when someone leaves the field they remember how delicious a fresh piece of produce tasted, and when they find themselves needing to fill their refrigerator or purchase a meal that they harken back to that moment, shaping their buying decision. Know your farmer, know your food.

503-852-1031
plateandpitchfork.com

A beautiful beet salad, fresh from the farm.

Beloved pop-up becomes a two-in-one restaurant.

Today, Portland has a handful of soul-satisfying southern restaurants from which to choose. But perhaps the most inspired wasn't a restaurant at all until 2018. Maya Lovelace's greatest inspiration as a chef is her grandma, Mae Lovelace. When Maya was a child growing up outside of Hickory, North Carolina, visits to grandma's house were her favorite part of the holidays. She would spend hours on a stepstool next to her, learning to make yeast rolls, fry in a cast-iron skillet, and frost cakes. Mae also served as entrepreneurial inspiration, running a cake business out of her home. Maya has fond memories of sitting at her grandma's kitchen table, watching her work, and listening to the whirring of her two KitchenAid mixers, both of which seemed to be constantly running. Lovelace has kept those memories close to heart throughout her time working in restaurants, even when she tried to distance herself from southern cuisine.

Lovelace got her first restaurant job at the age of seventeen and has stayed the course. But the time spent working at Husk in

> "We're really excited to bring this style of food to Portland–cornmeal fried catfish, hushpuppies, hoppin' john, country ham braised lima beans, banana pudding, all the good stuff. We hope that Yonder will serve as a kind of front porch for our neighborhood, a place for folks to sit with a glass of sweet tea and watch the traffic go by. Mae will evolve, letting us delve deeper into old recipe books and classic southern Appalachian foodways."
>
> –Maya Lovelace, Chef/Co-Owner, Mae/Yonder

Left: Maya Lovelace and Co-Owner Zach Lefler.
Right: Dipped Chicken.

Charleston, South Carolina, under Chef Sean Brock, helped rekindle her love of grandma's cooking and inspired her own obsession with heirloom produce and heritage recipes. Lovelace moved from Charleston to Portland, bringing her passion for southern ingredients and technique with her. Three years later, she started a pop-up named in her grandmother's honor. Mae became a twice-weekly pop-up celebrating Lovelace's southern heritage as well as the tremendous natural bounty of the Pacific Northwest. Cooking out of the backroom of the Old Salt Marketplace, Lovelace—along with Co-Owner Zach Lefler—provide a dinner service that focuses not only on delicious dishes, but also on the stories that inspire them. Lovelace personally serves every table, explaining the dish and the inspiration behind it, while sharing personal anecdotes and memories from childhood. The emphasis on human emotion and storytelling, combined with outstanding southern-inspired fare, has placed Mae in an elevated space that it alone occupies. Lovelace and Lefler are currently in the process of opening two restaurants inside one space. Mae will continue in a private, intimate dining room as a communal supper experience, while the new concept, Yonder, will help make the food a bit more accessible, offering Portlanders the Mae take on classic southern meats. Grandma Mae would be proud.

4636 Northeast 42nd Ave.
maepdx.com

The best bratwurst in Portland served out of the last original food cart at the 10th and Alder pod.

The last original food cart at the legendary 10th and Alder pod has stood the test of time for one reason: bratwurst. When George Wittkopp and his family moved west from Wisconsin to Portland, he couldn't find German sausage that met muster. So he went to the drawing board—experimenting with family recipes that date back to their homeland of Altengartz, Germany, along with the finest Northwest ingredients he could find. After years of trial and error, he thought he had nailed it, and Portland agreed. The Altengartz food cart has thrived since the year 2000, thanks in large part to the perfect blend of old country recipe and premium cuts of pork from Carlton Farms. George's son, Jameson, has been an almost omnipresent, driving, and visionary force for the business. And now a second cart resides at the new Beaverton food cart pod, BG Food Cartel. All the traditional sausage toppings are available, but don't overdo it. Let that sausage do the talking.

999 Southwest Alder St.
503-699-4962
germanbratwurst.com

Left: Jameson at the new Beaverton location.

Right: Jameson at the original 10th & Alder cart.

An ingredient-driven American bistro in the heart of Mississippi Avenue.

A *quaintrelle* is a woman who emphasizes a life of passion expressed through personal style, leisurely pastimes, charm, and a cultivation of life's pleasures. A finer name for a Portland restaurant has yet to be discovered. This neighborhood bistro excels in all aspects of a good restaurant—service, surroundings, beverages, and food. Which makes sense, given the team behind it. A food-loving ownership trio that also recently purchased the Abbey Road Farm, they bring strong management for the wine, front of house, and cocktail programs. A talented, self-taught chef who has worked in more elite Portland kitchens than perhaps anyone completes the talented group.

Bill Wallender grew up in North Dakota. He had family in Portland, and he would occasionally come out for summer visits. He moved to Spokane at the age of twenty-three to work, but he kept up the tradition of the occasional trip to Stumptown. When the allure of the big, or bigger, city was too much, he packed up and headed west. Lying on his application, the young man with little experience and no culinary training to speak of landed a job at Portland's oldest restaurant, Huber's. From there, he moved on to another iconic kitchen at Southpark Seafood. After two years there,

The owners of Quaintrelle have been lovingly renovating Abbey Road Farm in Yamhill County. In addition to being an event space and B&B, the farm will also grow food specifically for Quaintrelle. Local sommelier James Rahn is taking over the vineyard to focus on lesser-known grapes that supplement the restaurant's inventive wine program.

Left: Chef de Cuisine Bill Wallender leads the charge at dinner service.

Right: A sampling of seasonal dishes at Quaintrelle.

Wallender, wanting to try his hand at something smaller and more elaborate, moved on to work at Clarklewis while simultaneously pulling staging shifts at Le Pigeon. He took a brief sabbatical to be with his dying grandmother in North Dakota, and when he returned, he helped open the new Portland seafood staple, Cabezon. He would once again work for Chef Gabriel Rucker at Little Bird, followed by Chef Jenn Louis at the Sunshine Tavern, and capped off his pre-Quaintrelle career with a three-year run under Chef Joshua McFadden at Ava Gene's. Now in charge of his own kitchen, Wallender has made good use of his connections with local farmers and put his own spin on the region's bounty. Two years into the life of the restaurant, Quaintrelle is a standout on Mississippi Avenue. It's still a neighborhood bistro, just one that many of us are willing to leave our own to get to.

3936 North Mississippi Ave.
503-200-5787
quaintrelle.com

Modern, seasonal Israeli food interpreted by one of Portland's top chefs.

The term "Celebrity Chef" gets thrown around a lot, but in the case of Jenn Louis, there's some gravitas behind it. *Food & Wine Magazine* named her Chef of the Year in 2012, a handful of years after she opened her flagship restaurant, Lincoln. The hits kept coming, however, with a pair of James Beard Award nominations for Best Chef Northwest and an appearance on *Top Chef Masters*. On the heels of Lincoln's success, she opened the Sunshine Tavern and all was right with the world. Then she shook things up.

Jenn Louis was a creative child without a satisfactory artistic outlet. When she started cooking for herself in college, she took to it like a duck to water and discovered her calling. After college, Louis spent time in Israel working on a kibbutz. That experience left strong impressions on her. She eventually moved to Portland, went to culinary school, and opened her own catering business. Emboldened by her success, she opened Lincoln in 2008—a cornerstone of the North Williams Avenue culinary uprising. With inventive, seasonal offerings and stellar craft cocktails, Lincoln was a key contributor to Portland's ever-improving reputation as a culinary powerhouse.

But Louis is a chef who likes to have a hand in all aspects of her business. As 2016 was drawing to a close, she sold the Sunshine

Chef Louis is also an accomplished cookbook author. Her 2015 book, *Pasta by Hand*, was nominated for an International Association of Culinary Professionals award. Her second book, *The Book of Greens*, was released in spring 2017.

Left: The dining room at Ray.

Right: A wide array of offerings at Ray.

Tavern to be more present at Lincoln. She's also creative. Feeling bored culinarily, she decided in March 2017 to shutter Lincoln for good. In the span of a week, she open a new restaurant, Ray, in the same space. No small undertaking. Wanting something lighter and more fun, and sensing a shift in people's dining habits, Ray was a natural progression.

Louis envisions the future of Portland cuisine as taking farm-to-table to the next level by having a better understanding of ingredients, how to develop those flavors, and how to take advantage of increased access to imports. Ray appears to fit into that notion perfectly, offering a modern interpretation on Israeli cuisine and its many influences. The dishes are lively and full-flavored. The atmosphere is warm and convivial. The menu is seasonal—with plenty of vegetables, colorful salads, inventive takes on proteins, and, thankfully, shakshuka. Ray's future looks bright. But we'll have to wait and see where inspiration leads Chef Louis a decade from now.

3808 North Williams Ave.
503-288-6200
raypdx.com

The only place in the country for Mauritian food.

The food carts in Portland are a dream come true for those looking to broaden their culinary horizons. With the carts serving predominantly ethnic food, you can get an authentic Polish pierogi, a plate of Indian chicken tikka masala, and a Chinese jianbing within a fifty-foot walk. The variety is staggering, bordering on intimidating at times. Almost every type of cuisine is represented, including Mauritian food at Chez Dodo.

According to Chef/Owner Shyam Dausoa, Chez Dodo is the only Mauritian food cart—or restaurant, for that matter—in the United States. Which is difficult to believe, given how good the food is. The small island nation of Mauritius, located east of Madagascar in the Indian Ocean, draws culinary influence from India, France, China, and Africa, among some others. One standout in particular: the Shyamosa. The chef's namesake offering is a samosa on steroids: a massive fried pastry stuffed with spiced potato and vegetables, topped with a blend of mint-cilantro chutney and sweet chili sauces.

The original Chez Dodo cart at the Southwest 5th and Stark pod suffered extensive damage when a tree limb fell on its roof during a 2017 snow storm. But a "Go Fund Me" page and the support of a rabid fan base brought the cart back to life. Chef Shyam has even added a second cart location in Happy Valley.

Top left: Dholl Puri, filled Mauritian flatbread.

Top right: Mine Frire, Mauritian fried noodles.

Above: Chef Shyam Dausoa in front of the downtown cart.

427 Southwest Stark St., Downtown
503-270-9258

13551 Southeast 145th Ave., Happy Valley
chezdodopdx.net

Legenday chef and Portland culinary royalty.

If there was a Mount Rushmore dedicated to the culinary legends of Portland, strong arguments could be made for the inclusion of at least five to ten chefs. But no pundit would deny the inclusion of Vitaly Paley. The James Beard Award winner for Best Chef Northwest in 2005 has also been in the running for Beard-related hardware four other times. Not only is Paley responsible for three of the city's most highly regarded restaurants, but he also helped groom a number of talented chefs who have gone on to become shining stars in their own right.

Paley was born near Kiev in the former Soviet Union and immigrated to New York in the 1970s, thanks to the piano prodigy's full-ride scholarship to Juilliard. After two years at the prestigious school, Paley, feeling he didn't want to set his career path in concrete just yet, left Juilliard and started working in restaurants around New York. He stuck with it. Paley would attend the French Culinary Institute in New York before ascending the ranks in the field, working at Union Square Café, Remi, and Chanterelle. He then apprenticed at Moulin de la Gorce, a two-starred Michelin restaurant in France, before returning to New York.

However, a seed was planted while Paley was cooking abroad. In a now-famous anecdote, Paley recalls the time that the kitchen received a basket of the most flavorful and complex morel

As if a James Beard Award wasn't enough, Chef Paley is also an *Iron Chef America* Champion. In 2011, he dispatched Iron Chef Jose Garces in Battle Radish on the popular Food Network show.

Left: A sampling of dishes at Paley's newest restaurant, Headwaters.

Center: Cooking with fire at the Imperial.

Right: New York–style pizza at the Crown.

mushrooms he had ever encountered. Paley asked from what part of France the mushrooms were sourced. He was somewhat perplexed but even more intrigued when the answer came back, "Oregon." At the time, Paley was looking to push his cuisine forward by being close to the source of his ingredients. The more he researched, the more the Willamette Valley looked like it should be home. Shortly thereafter, Paley and his wife, Kimberly, a front-of-house dynamo, moved to Portland. They eventually found a cafe space on Northwest 21st Avenue that was perfect, and in 1995 they opened Paley's Place, a world-class neighborhood bistro. In 2012 they opened the Imperial, a wood-fired and rotisserie-focused restaurant that expanded into breakfast and lunch territory. Then, returning to Vitaly's Russian roots, in 2016 the Paleys opened Headwaters in the Heathman Hotel. The space that had once been occupied by the legendary Heathman Restaurant and Bar is now fittingly overseen by Paley. Finally, in 2017 the Paleys revamped the bar next door to the Imperial into a casual cocktail bar serving New York–style pizza, called the Crown. Also quite fitting.

Paley's Place, 1204 Northwest 21st Ave., 503-243-2403, paleysplace.net

The Imperial, 410 Southwest Broadway, 503-228-7222, imperialpdx.com

Headwaters, 1001 Southwest Broadway, 503-790-7752, headwaterspdx.com

The Crown, 410 Southwest Broadway, 503-228-7224, imperialpdx.comthe-crown

Great food and drink without a big-name chef or deep pockets.

Jennifer Cale and Kara Lammerman know a thing or two about tending bar in Portland. Individually, the two friends have been pouring pints at various watering holes for years—and dreaming of a day when they might do so at their own establishment. Luckily, in a mid-sized market like Portland, dreams like those can still come true. It was no easy task, however. The right place, the right time, the right price—a lot of things have to come together when you don't have big investors behind you. But then a Craigslist ad that was up for just one day caught Lammerman's eye. She tracked down the posting party and the property to an unassuming pizzeria in Northeast Portland. The space wasn't big, and it needed a woman's touch—or rather, two women's touch—to transform it. But it was the right fit, and they pounced.

Two years later, the Pocket Pub has become a neighborhood favorite, giving equal time to families, couples, and barstool regulars. Not wanting to reinvent the wheel, Cale and Lammerman kept the pizza oven. Then, utilizing the collective culinary strengths and

With just about everybody on payroll adding a flourish until the final product was ready for the world, the elevated poppers at the Pocket Pub are a prime example of the staff's collaborative strength—jalapeno stuffed with cream cheese and apple, wrapped in prosciutto, and finished with a drizzle of honey.

Above left: Outside, looking in.

Top right: Inside, looking out.

Above right: The elevated poppers: stuffed jalapeno with cream cheese, apple, prosciutto, and honey drizzle.

palates of the staff, they put together a strong menu anchored by some of the best pizza in Portland. As you might imagine, the drinks are no slouch either.

2719 Northeast 7th Ave.
503-287-3645
pocketpubpdx.com

The Northwest's leading purveyor and proponent of specialty game meat.

In 1990, Geoff Latham founded Nicky USA to fill a void in the Northwest culinary landscape—game meat. Specifically, locally raised rabbit, quail, elk, fallow venison, goose, goat, veal, water buffalo, venison, and American bison. Today, Nicky USA has become the Northwest's leading butcher and purveyor of specialty game and high-quality meat, offering more than five hundred products, with exotic game selections expanding to include yak, caribou, antelope, python, kangaroo, emu, and ostrich. Based in Portland, one of Latham's goals is to create relationships with local and international ranchers, as well as James Beard Award–winning chefs, to make game a mainstay of specialty markets and a standard offering in fine restaurants. The company recently purchased its own forty-acre farm to raise game and host friends and customers. It also created the nation's only USDA-compliant mobile processing units for the sustainable and humane processing of animals. Nicky USA expanded in 2013, adding a second location in Seattle and proving that game meat in the Northwest has staying power.

Nicky USA's Wild About Game is an annual celebration of game meat that gathers some of the best chefs in the Pacific Northwest for a head-to-head cooking competition, along with ranchers, farmers, and purveyors for a day of cooking competitions and tastings. The event takes place on Oregon's Mt. Hood in the autumn, and it includes the Artisan Marketplace, a showcase of local artisan products and purveyors, as well as Nicky Farms proteins and meats from Nicky USA's family of meat producers.

Above left: A creative offering from the Wild About Game competition.

Top right: A number of Portland's best chefs now use game meats from Nicky USA in their menu offerings.

Above right: Dinner at a Nicky USA farm event.

223 Southeast 3rd Ave.
503-243-4263
nickyusa.com

REVEREND NAT'S HARD CIDER

One of the country's most experimental cideries—and Portland's favorite.

When Nat West decided to start making cider thirteen years ago, he had no idea what he was doing. That turned out to be a good thing. Back then, West was a part-time stay-at-home dad running a CSA across the street from his house. One of his friends had a large apple tree in the yard that was producing a lot of fruit. To mitigate waste, West and his friends made a litany of apple-based edibles: pies, apple butter, applesauce. But there was still a ton of leftover apples. West thought cider seemed like a solid plan. So, he Googled how to make a cider press, put one together from equipment he had lying around the house, and he was off to the races. West knew what hard apple cider was in the abstract, but he had never actually consumed the product. So a lot of on-the-job-training was involved. As luck would have it, West's family hosted a weekly neighborhood potluck on Wednesdays, and some of the neighbors were homebrewers. They suggested using beer yeast in his cider, and West gave it a shot. Not knowing what he didn't know, but being a natural with flavor profiles, West used yeast and unconventional ingredients to yield ciders that were completely outside of the norm—and also delicious.

West got ordained to marry some friends of his around the time he started making cider. The moniker "Reverend Nat" was kind of a joke when he started bottling and labeling, but it had a nice ring to it, and it wound up sticking.

Left: Bottles for purchase at the taproom.
Right: Nat West.

West soon became the belle of the ball at the weekly potlucks, drawing an ever-expanding number of "neighbors" who were there to try the cider they kept hearing about. Around this time, West started sampling commercially available ciders and was, more often than not, disappointed. So he became fully licensed and produced what he thought would be enough cider for his first year of business, two thousand gallons. He sold out in two months. In 2013, he moved the business into a larger warehouse space that included a taproom. Once he had explored the space, his creativity flourished. Belgian ale spices, fresh Northwest hops, local fruit juices, barrel aging, wild fermentation—West's repertoire of methods and ingredients continued to expand, along with the product's popularity. In 2018, he added another, larger facility in an attempt to do something the business hadn't accomplished since its inception—meet his distributors' volume demands. "It's a good problem to have" notes West. "But it's still a problem."

1813 Northeast 2nd Ave.
503-567-2221
reverendnatshardcider.com

A renowned charcuterie and restaurant combination looking to the past to move Portland's cuisine into the future.

Elias Cairo and his sister, Michelle, grew up in about as bucolic a setting as you'll find. His father moved to America from Greece, eventually establishing a family farm in a tranquil valley outside of Salt Lake City, Utah. In addition to running two restaurants, his father made charcuterie at home. This approach was only bolstered after Elias moved to Europe to pursue a culinary career. He apprenticed in Switzerland for five years under Masterchef Annegret Schlumpf. There, everybody was an artisan—everything was made by hand and from scratch, using techniques and traditions that date back centuries. The experience had a lasting effect. He gained some experience working in Greece before moving back to Switzerland. Then he visited Michelle, who was living in Portland.

After a stroll through the Portland Farmers Market, Cairo had two takeaways: The bounty of the area was world-class, and there was no salami. Not long after that fateful visit, Elias moved to Portland and began working around the city, landing at Castagna and working his way up to executive chef. There, he met Castagna's manager, Nate Tilden. Tilden would also open the iconic restaurant Clyde Commons in 2007. One night over a beer, Tilden mentioned to

OP Wurst is an offshoot of "Frankfurter Fridays" at the Olympia Provisions restaurants. Now with three locations and a hot dog cart, the classic American hot dogs on steroids created by frankfurter mastermind Victor Deras have garnered their own cult following.

Left: Charcuterie Board.

Right: A small handful of restaurants/stands around town allow the uninitiated to sample the wares.

Cairo that he wanted to open a restaurant featuring charcuterie. And that was that. In 2009, Olympia Provisions became Oregon's first USDA-approved salumeria.

Sourcing only the finest local ingredients he could find and using the old-world techniques that were the foundation of his ethos, Cairo's meat products earned almost instant recognition. Alex Yoder, who also worked at Castagna, and Clyde Commons took the reigns as executive chef of the restaurant side in 2010, and everything was in place for Olympia Provisions' rise to greatness. The first year they entered the Good Food Awards, they took home four awards, more than anyone else. Then Olympia Provisions products landed a coveted spot on Oprah's Favorite Things list, and the restaurant's status as a local legend was cemented. But Oprah accolades aside, OP remains unmatched in quality, earning an equally unparalleled reputation among artisans in the Northwest and beyond. With potential plans to acquire a farm and slaughterhouse, it doesn't look like that reputation will be going anywhere soon.

Southeast
107 Southeast Washington St.
503-954-3663

Northwest
1632 Northwest Thurman St.
503-894-8136
olympiaprovisions.com

NEW DEAL DISTILLERY

Blazing a path for craft distillers in Portland and beyond.

From humble beginnings as perhaps the smallest licensed distillery in America, what founder Tom Burkleaux started in 2004 helped launch an industry in the Portland area. Distilleries making everything from aquavit to whiskey bloomed up around his New Deal Distillery, forming Portland's Distillery Row. With well over a dozen craft distilleries in town, Portland is now one of the premier cities in America for distilled spirits. And New Deal exemplifies the Portland ethos in its approach. One of New Deal's slogans is "MADE RIGHT, MADE RIGHT HERE." An apt description. All of New Deal's spirits are made onsite at the distillery in Southeast Portland, with special pride taken in the high-quality ingredients used in the process. For example, the fresh organic ginger root in the New Deal Ginger Liqueur, 100 percent estate-grown Hood River Bartlett pears for the New Deal Pear Brandy, soft white Oregon wheat in the New Deal Vodka, and locally roasted coffee from Water Avenue for the Coffee Liqueur. New Deal is also perhaps the largest local distillery that hasn't been fueled by outside investor money. It takes pride in giving back to the community and doing things the right way, making spirits in the truest spirit of the city.

"I believe the craft distilling industry couldn't exist without craft breweries and all the local and farm-to-table movements in food. Also, the appreciation of artisan and craft you find in cities like Portland. Without them, our customers wouldn't exist."–Tom Burkleaux, founder, New Deal Distillery

Top: Some of the offerings from New Deal Distillery. Photo courtesy of New Deal Distillery.

Above left: The distillery itself. Photo courtesy of New Deal Distillery.

Above right: Founder, Tom Burkleaux. Photo courtesy of New Deal Distillery.

900 Southeast Salmon St.
503-234-2513
newdealdistillery.com

Vegetable-driven, Middle Eastern–inspired cuisine on East Burnside.

Sam Smith is no stranger to Middle Eastern flavor profiles, or running a top-flight restaurant, for that matter. Having honed his craft with business partner Michael Solomonov at Philadelphia's acclaimed Israeli-inspired Zahav, Smith moved to Portland and helped open one of the city's most widely loved Italian restaurants, Ava Gene's. With Tusk, Smith finds himself once again focused on Middle Eastern flavors, while also paying careful attention to the changing seasons.

In addition to seasonality, how and where ingredients are sourced carries weight for Smith. He's developed close relationships with a number of area farms over the years, and all of the restaurant's vegetables, along with most flours and grains, can be traced back to those associations. "We are definitely vegetable focused, but do not consider ourselves a vegetarian restaurant. A lot of our menu is vegan, gluten free, dairy free, but not limiting to people that don't have dietary restrictions," says Smith. And while vegetables tend to do most of the heavy lifting on the menu, there are enough meat and fish options to satiate meat lovers.

The seasonal focus expands beyond the mains, however. Former Le Pigeon pastry chef Nora Antene and Bar Manager Tony Contreras produce desserts and cocktails that are just as in keeping with the time of year as the primary courses.

The dining room is bright, open, and lively, and dishes are meant to be shared. Chef Smith sums it up: "The dining experience is really fun and interactive. We don't do traditional coursing, but rather overlap all of the food, trying to get as much on the table at once. My favorite part about dining at Tusk is the way all of the food goes

Top: The dining room at Tusk. Photo courtesy of A. J. Meeker.

Above left: Herb Salad. Photo courtesy of A. J. Meeker.

Above center: Barley Salad. Photo courtesy of A. J. Meeker.

Above right: Hummus with peppers and chickpeas. Photo courtesy of A. J. Meeker.

together, creating a sum that is greater than its parts. And there are no rules about how you have to eat it, making each diner's experience singular." The culinary community beyond Portland has taken notice. Despite only having been open since summer 2016, *Food & Wine Magazine* named Tusk a Restaurant of the Year in 2017. The same year, it earned a spot as one of *Bon Appétit*'s 50 Best New Restaurants. According to Smith, "Tusk is the culmination of my love for the food I made with Michael, combined with the incredible products of the Pacific Northwest."

2448 East Burnside St., 503-894-8082
tuskpdx.com

One of the city's favorite burrito shops and a family success story.

David Canales arrived in Los Angeles from Mexico in the late '60s. In 1970, he landed a job in the kitchen of Garduno's. During the course of his multi-decade tenure at the legendary Mexican food eatery, he learned everything he could about running a restaurant, including the recipes, ingredients, and techniques that produce authentic East L.A. Mexican food. His nephews came up to Portland to open their own restaurant, Burrito Loco, in the early '90s. When they needed reinforcements, Canales brought up the rest of the family. With everything running smoothly, he opened his own restaurant, King Burrito, in 1995. Putting everything he had learned over the years into his own business, King Burrito brought an authenticity to North Portland that was unparalleled. And delicious. More than twenty years later, Canales still opens the restaurant every day and runs the kitchen along with his wife and three children. And while the neighborhood's demographics have changed over the years, almost nothing has at King Burrito. And the city of Portland couldn't be happier about it.

2924 North Lombard St.
503-283-9757
kingburritomexicanfood.com

The namesake King Burrito is a large flour tortilla filled with refried beans, a chile relleno, steak picado, and a homemade avocado sauce. In addition to being a local favorite for two-plus decades, students at the nearby University of Portland have been using it as a hangover cure for just as long.

Top: Outside of King Burrito.

Above: Inside King Burrito.

More than a century of fresh-baked bread at the heart of Portland's culinary culture.

Like Powell's Books or Forest Park, the Franz Bakery is an iconic component of Portland's cultural identity. If you've spent any time in the city, you've almost undoubtedly sampled some of the bakery's handiwork. And if you've ever driven past 340 Northeast 11th Avenue, you've encountered the unmistakable wafting aroma of Franz fresh-baked bread. In 1906, Engelbert Franz immigrated to the United States from Austria. He was joined soon after by his brother, Joe, and together they founded the bakery that would ultimately be known as Franz. In the 1920s they began delivering bread to Portlanders by horse-drawn wagons. They added their iconic spinning loaf to the bakery roof in 1956 to celebrate Franz's 50th anniversary. And to celebrate its 100th anniversary, Franz upped the bakery's game by setting the Guinness World Record for the longest hot dog bun, at 104 feet, 9½ inches.

Beyond the Portland community, Franz made a lasting culinary contribution to the world by developing the first uniform five-inch hamburger bun in 1926. The bakery has also stayed current by launching a certified organic line of breads in 2010. And most

> In summer 2016, Franz launched the "Get Portland Baked Grilled Cheese Machine." In an act of goodwill, the converted route truck drives around the Portland area serving complimentary grilled cheese sandwiches. As you might have guessed, the colorful, ubiquitous truck has become a welcomed sight wherever it's spotted.

Top left: The iconic spinning loaf, added for the bakery's 50th anniversary.

Top right: Turkey sandwich on Franz bread.

Above: The uniform 5-inch hamburger bun, developed by Franz.

recently in 2012, they added gluten-free products to the stable. Today, the Franz Bakery is in its fourth generation of family ownership, with nine bakeries throughout the Northwest.

340 Northeast 11th St.
503-232-2191
franzbakery.com

The confluence of hip hop & soul food, and the culmination of a dream.

Longtime music producer, singer/songwriter, and promoter William Travis III, aka Dub, is as talented behind the line as he is in the studio. So in keeping, Dub opened a catering business in 2010. Then in 2012, along with business partner and Portland hip hop pioneer James McClendon, he opened Mac & Dub's Excellent Chicken and Waffles. At the same time, the two formed a new group called Mac & Dub and the Smoking Section, which played out regularly, including a weekly gig at Plew's Taphouse in St. Johns. When an arsonist torched the new chicken and waffle restaurant along with the attached music studio, Plew's owner, Randy Plew, told Dub that a dive bar down the street had a kitchen that was no longer being used. Not prone to giving up, in 2013 the chicken and waffle joint was reborn as Dub's, a small soul food restaurant in the Ranger Tavern.

Portlanders have a way of sussing out and touting the real deal. Word spread quickly, and every time Dub was about to invest in advertising, his restaurant made a new Top 10 list. Then, in 2017, a brick-and-mortar location too good to pass on and just down the street in the heart of St. Johns became available. Dub pounced. On New Year's Eve, 2018, Dub's St. Johns opened with a party featuring plenty of soul food and live music. As deft as he is at crafting a melody or composing lyrics, some words never found their way into Dub's repertoire. Like "quit," for example.

8537 North Lombard St.
503-998-8230
dubstjohns.com

Top left: Lunchtime at Dub's.

Top right: Chicken and soul food sides.

Above: Fried catfish platter.

A story every bit as good as its namesake Thai chicken and rice dish.

Narumol (Nong) Poonsukwattana came to Portland from Bangkok in 2003 at the age of twenty-three with seventy dollars and two suitcases. She worked at a number of restaurants in town, including perhaps the most well known Thai restaurant in the city, Pok Pok. Wanting to do her own thing, but also knowing that Thai food in the city was becoming extremely competitive, she decided to open a food cart that would focus on the mastery of a single dish—Khao Man Gai. In 2009, armed with her mother's recipe and the knowledge that Americans love chicken, she opened the Khao Man Gai food cart at the legendary 10th and Alder pod downtown. She bought only the best ingredients available and painstakingly produced the chicken, rice, and pungeon sauce that turned Portland on its ear. In accordance with tradition, the chicken dish comes with cucumbers and cilantro, and it is followed by a cup of palate-cleansing soup. The perfectly balanced plate of food became so popular that additional cart locations would follow. Nong's American dream culminated with the opening of her own brick-and-mortar restaurant in 2014, and a second location downtown in 2018.

1003 Southwest Alder St. (Original cart location)
971-255-3480
khaomangai.com

Nong's pungeon sauce became so popular that it is now bottled and sold in stores. The flavorful and complex sauce comprised of fermented soy bean puree mixed with garlic, ginger, thai chilies, vinegar, and sugar, should be avoided at all costs by those with a history of addiction.

Top: A plate of Khao Man Gai.

Above left: Poonsukwattana Nong, in front of the original food cart.

Above right: Nong at her first restaurant location.

An out-of-the way Mt. Tabor space becomes one of Portland's most exciting new restaurants.

Not content to be just another stellar farm-to-table standby, Coquine is an ambitious, French-inspired restaurant that is pushing the city's cuisine forward. But this is Portland, so the restaurant is warm, welcoming, and unpretentious. Katy Millard was born in Zimbabwe to Portuguese parents. She spent her childhood in Alabama and New Orleans, being influenced by wide-ranging regional cuisine as well as both parents' proclivity for home cooking. Millard trained in Paris and went on to work in some of the most well respected restaurants around, including Guy Savoy in Paris, Mirabeau in Monaco, Le Château de la Chèvre d'Or in Eze, and Coi in San Francisco. In 2010, she moved to Portland, where she worked in several respected kitchens, including Bollywood Theater, Sauvage, and the Woodsman Tavern. She also met the man who would become her husband, Ksandek Podbielski. As fate would have it, Podbielski is as accomplished at front-of-house hospitality and wine pairing as Millard is in the kitchen.

Within six months of opening, Coquine won Rising Star Restaurant of the Year from *Portland Monthly Magazine*, Restaurant

The French word *coquine* is a lighthearted chide for a mischievous little girl or something a bit more flirtatious when addressing an adult. Coquine, the restaurant, lives up to the definition of the word with a location, ambiance, drinks, and cuisine that emanate charm and confidence but always with a playful wink.

Above left: Co-Owner Ksandek Podbielski and Co-Owner/Chef Katy Millard.

Top right: An exemplary dish at Coquine.

Above right: The dining room at Coquine.

of the Year from Eater, and earned a three-star review from the *Oregonian*. Since then, Coquine has been recognized by *Bon Appétit* as one of America's Best New Restaurants 2016, *Wine Enthusiast* as one of America's 100 Best Wine Restaurants of 2016, and has been nominated for two James Beard Awards for Best New Restaurant 2016 and Best Chef Northwest in 2017.

6839 Southeast Belmont St.
503-384-2483

Portland's go-to provider for microgreens and edible flowers.

There are plenty of farms in and around Portland producing a seemingly endless parade of organic and heirloom fruits and vegetables. But if you've been paying attention to plate composition in recent years, some more delicate but critical accoutrements are helping to bring it all together. In Portland, that's where Nathan Gilds comes in. After years of studying horticulture, growing hobby plants, and working in the horticulture industry, Gilds wanted to apply his knowledge towards a career. When a chef friend told Gilds about microgreens and the demand for them from Portland's most innovative chefs, a new career path presented itself.

Working closely with and catering to the needs of the city's chefs, Gilds grows more than twenty varieties of microgreens and edible flowers, coming into heavy rotation in spring and summer. If a chef wants to use a certain microgreen, and even if Gilded Greens hasn't produced it, they'll track down the seeds, figure out how to grow it, and accommodate the chef's creativity in any way they can.

503-756-3566
gildedgreenspdx.com

"We're small, and we care. After years of working for other people, Nate's devotion to providing high-quality microgreens to Portland's chefs is evident in not only in our products, but his interactions with the companies we work with."–Karen Locke, Marketing Strategy & Sales for Gilded Greens

Top left: Nathan Gilds.

Top right: Watermelon steak with microgreen and edible flower. Courtesy of Waz Wu.

Above: Micro pea tendril.

Plates of goodness and a dog-friendly atmosphere create a Portland favorite.

Good instincts and natural talent can take you a long way. You can train and practice all you want, but it wasn't hours spent looking at diagrams of the triangle offense that allowed Michal Jordan to sink shots from the free-throw line. Similarly, Janette Kaden didn't go to the Culinary Institute of America or study real estate theory. But she has an inherent acumen for both, and it's possibly genetic. Her grandfather started the Kissin' Cousins Diner in Seaside in the '50s. When a new cook would ask how much pastrami needed to be put in the Rueben, the answer was always, "until it looks like a lot." That sort of outlook will earn you points with the public.

When Kaden and business partner Christie Griffin saw the "for lease" sign up in a coffee shop on Northeast Alberta, they snagged it. Instinct told Kaden that it was a good location for a restaurant. And despite the fact that she had no culinary training, she knew how to put "goodness" on a plate. Since their opening in 2002, the Tin Shed has been one of the most popular restaurants in Northeast, providing good energy and good farm-to-table food for the good people of Portland.

> The Tin Shed has a well-earned reputation for being one of the most dog-friendly restaurants in Portland. In addition to welcoming dogs anytime, the cafe provides a fido-friendly menu, and every Tuesday after 3 p.m. is Dog Lovers Night– where every regularly priced adult meal purchased earns a free pet meal.

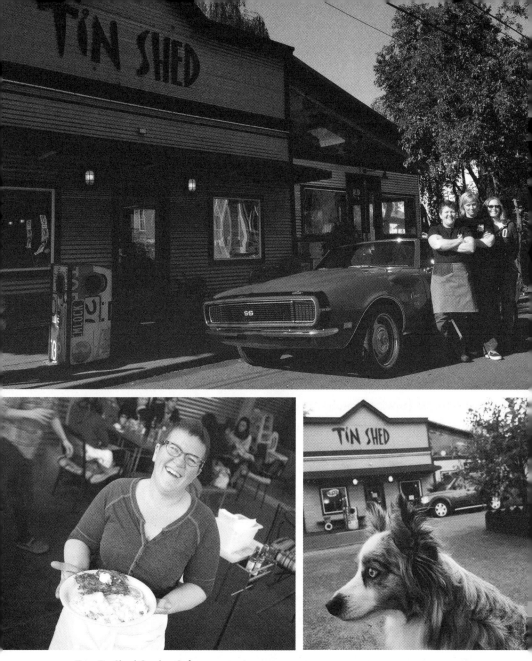

Top: Tin Shed Garden Cafe.

Above left: Janette Kaden with a plate of goodness.

Above right: Dog Lovers Night, every Tuesday.

1438 Northeast Alberta St.
503-288-6966
tinshedgardencafe.com

The best in indie music, a hotel next door, and new menus put the Doug Fir Lounge on the Portland map.

Drawing equal parts curious out of towners and locals alike, the Doug Fir Lounge has been one of Portland's hottest hot spots since opening in 2004. Coming from the worlds of architecture, music, and fashion, founders Jeff Kovel, Mike Quinn, and John Plummer wanted to open a world-class establishment that showcased the best Portland has to offer. With a full-service restaurant, an intimate craft cocktail bar, an outdoor patio bar, a state-of-the-art live music venue with nightly shows downstairs, and the boutique Jupiter Hotel next door, they did just that. The lounge's unique design is reminiscent of a space-age log cabin in the woods, but on East Burnside. Everything is custom, and it feels like it. The Doug Fir's ambience is complemented by a rejuvenated food and drink menu from new Head Chef Kevin Rubis and Bar Manager Peter Carpenter that is fresh and ingredient-driven, but still in the comfort food pocket.

830 East Burnside St.
503-231-9663
dougfirlounge.com

The music venue at the Doug Fir is more than a stage for local bands to hone their craft. The nightly lineup regularly features some of the world's most renown indie acts and touring musicians.

Top: A new northwest ingredient-driven menu from Head Chef Kevin Rubis debuted in 2018.

Above left: The inviting South Bar at the Doug Fir Lounge.

Above right: The selfie-worthy moose.

Premium local ingredients along with some considerable imagination combined to make an ice cream shop with a cult following.

They certainly could not have known it at the time, but when cousins Kim and Tyler Malek decided to open an ice cream cart in early 2011 it was the birth of a cult empire. Since that time, Salt & Straw has grown into the largest small batch ice cream company in the world, with locations in Portland, Seattle, Los Angeles, and San Francisco. Though the availability and distribution of the line-inducing product casts a further net. The handcrafted, chef-driven ice cream flavors utilize ingredients that are sourced locally, seasonally, and sustainably. They also collaborate with other local artisans to create one of a kind classic and occasionally boundary-pushing Portland flavors like Arbequina Olive Oil—produced with Red Ridge Farms, and the Pear & Blue Cheese—engineered with Oregon Trail Northwest Bartlett Pears and Rogue Creamery's Crater Lake Blue Cheese. The line to acquire a scoop or a pint can exceed an hour, depending on time of day and weather. And while some might scoff at the idea of queueing for ice cream, the faces of the freshley bestowed radiate with glib justification.

Left: Another happy customer. Photo courtesy of Leela Cydross.
Right: The Pear & Blue Chees ice cream.

2035 Northeast Alberta St.
503-208-3867

838 Northwest 23rd Ave.
971-271-8168

3345 Southeast Division St.
503-208-2054

Wiz Bang Bar
126 Southwest 2nd Ave.
503-384-2150
saltandstraw.com

RESTAURANTS A-Z

Andina
1314 Northwest Glisan St.

Ataula
1818 Northwest 23rd Pl.

Altengartz
999 Southwest Alder St.

Ava Gene's
3377 Southeast Division St.

Aviary
1733 Northeast Alberta St.

Aviv
1125 Southeast Division St.

Beast
5425 Northeast 30th Ave.

Besaw's
1545 Northwest 21st Ave.

Bistro Agnes
527 Southwest 12th Ave.

Bollywood Theater
2039 Northeast Alberta St.
3010 Southeast Division St.

Broder Cafe
2508 Southeast Clinton St.

Broder Nörd
2240 North Interstate Ave.

Broder Øst
102 Oak St. #100

Broder Söder
8800 Southwest Oleson Rd.

Burger Stevens
6328 Southwest Capitol Way,
701 Southwest 6th Ave.

Cabezon
5200 Northeast Sacramento St.

Cacao
414 Southwest 13th Ave.

Canton Grill
2610 Southeast 82nd Ave.

Castagna
1752 Southeast Hawthorne Blvd.

Chameleon Restaurant & Bar
2000 Northeast 40th Ave.

Cheese Bar
6031 Southeast Belmont St.

Chez Dodo (Downtown)
427 Southwest Stark St..

Chez Dodo (Happy Valley)
13551 Southeast 145th Ave.

Chizu
1126 Southwest Alder St.

Coquine
6839 Southeast Belmont St.

**Country Cat Dinner House
and Bar**
7937 Southeast Stark St.

Dan & Louis Oyster Bar
208 Southwest Ankeny St.

Departure
525 Southwest Morrison S.

Doug Fir Lounge
830 East Burnside St.

Dub's St. Johns
8537 North Lombard St.

Ecliptic Brewing
825 North Cook St.

Elephants Delicatessen
115 Northwest 22nd Ave.

Expatriate
5424 Northeast 30th Ave.

Farm Spirit
1414 Southeast Morrison St.

Franz Bakery
340 Northeast 11th St.

Grain & Gristle
1473 Northeast Prescott St.

Grassa
1205 Southwest Washington St.
1506 Northwest 23rd Ave.

Ha VL
2738 Southeast 82nd Ave.

**Hair of the Dog Brewing
Company**
61 Southeast Yamhill St.

Hale Pele
2733 Northeast Broadway

Han Oak
511 Northeast 24th Ave.

Hat Yai
1605 Northeast Killingsworth St.

Headwaters
1001 Southwest Broadway

Higgins
1239 Southwest Broadway

Holdfast
2133 Southeast 11th Ave.

Horse Brass Pub
4534 Southeast Belmont St.

Huber's
411 Southwest 3rd Ave.

Jackrabbit
830 Southwest 6th Ave.

Kachka
720 Southeast Grand Ave.

Ken's Artisan Bakery
338 Northwest 21st Ave.

Ken's Artisan Pizza
304 Southeast 28th Ave.

Kenny & Zuke's Delicatessen
1038 Southwest Stark St.

Kenny & Zuke's Bagelworks
2376 Northwest Thurman St.

Kim Jong Grillin'
4606 Southeast Division St.

Kim Jong Smokehouse
413 Northwest 21st Ave.
126 Southwest 2nd Ave.

King Burrito
2924 North Lombard St.

La Moule
2500 Southeast Clinton St.

Le Pigeon
738 East Burnside St.

Lardo
1212 SoutheastHawthorne Blvd.
1205 Southwest Washington St.

Laurelhurst Market
3155 East Burnside St.

Little Bird
215 Southwest 6th Ave.

Mae/Yonder
4636 Northeast 42nd Ave.

Mother's Bistro & Bar
212 Southwest Stark St.

My Father's Place
523 Southeast Grand Ave.

New Deal Distillery
900 Southeast Salmon St.

Nicky USA
223 Southeast 3rd Ave.

Nomad.PDX
575 Northeast 24th Ave.

Nong's Khao Man Gai
1003 Southwest Alder St.

Nudi Noodle Palace
4310 Southeast Woodstock Ave.

Old Town Pizza
226 Northwest Davis St.

Olympia Provisions
107 Southeast Washington St.
1632 Northwest Thurman St.

Oui Wine Bar & Restaurant
2425 Southeast 35th Pl.

Old Salt Marketplace
5027 Northeast 42nd Ave.

Ox
2225 Northeast Martin Luther King Jr. Blvd.

PaaDee/Langbaan
6 Southeast 28th Ave.

Paley's Place
1204 Northwest 21st Ave.

Pambiche
2811 Northeast Glisan St.

Plaza Del Toro
105 SoutheastTaylor St.

Pocket Pub
2719 Northeast 7th Ave.

Portland Farmers Markets
1831 Southwest Pedestrian Trail

Po'Shines Café De La Soul
8139 North Denver Ave.

Q
828 Southwest 2nd Ave.

Quaintrelle
3936 North Mississippi Ave.

Ray
3808 North Williams Ave.

Reverend Nat's Hard Cider
1813 Northeast 2nd Ave.

RingSide Fish House
838 Southwest Park Ave.

RingSide Steakhouse
2165 West Burnside St.

Roe
515 Southwest Broadway,
Ste. 100

Salt and Straw
2035 Northeast Alberta St.
838 Northwest 23rd Ave.
3345 Southeast Division St.

Saraveza
1004 North Killingsworth St.

Signal Station Pizza
8302 North Lombard St.

St. Honoré Boulangerie
2335 Northwest Thurman St.

St. Jack
1610 Northwest 23rd Ave.

Stacked Sandwiches
1643 Southeast 3rd Ave.

Stumptown Coffee Roasters
4525 Southeast Division St.

Tapalaya
28 Northeast 28th Ave.

Tails & Trotters
525 Northeast 28th Ave.

The Crown
410 Southwest Broadway

The Imperial
410 Southwest Broadway

The Sudra
2333 Northeast Glisan St.

The Umami Café
611 Southwest Kingston Ave.

Tin Shed Garden Café
1438 Northeast Alberta St.

Trifecta Tavern
726 Southeast 6th Ave.

Tusk
2448 East Burnside St.

Voodoo Doughnut
22 Southwest 3rd Ave.

Wiz Bang Bar
126 Southwest 2nd Ave.

APPENDIX

SOUTHEAST PORTLAND

NORTHEAST PORTLAND

NORTHWEST PORTLAND